Wisdom: The Good Life

Wisdom Literature and the Rule of Benedict

Irene Nowell, OSB

Foreword by
Abbot John Klassen, OSB

LITURGICAL PRESS
Collegeville, Minnesota

www.litpress.org

Scripture texts, prefaces, introductions, footnotes, and cross references used in this work are taken from the *New American Bible, revised edition*, © 2010, 1991, 1986, 1970 Confraternity of Christian Doctrine, Inc., Washington, DC. All rights reserved. No part of this work may be reproduced or transmitted in any form or by any means, electronic or mechanical, including photocopying, recording, or by any information storage and retrieval system, without permission in writing from the copyright owner.

1   2   3   4   5   6   7   8   9

Library of Congress Cataloging-in-Publication Data

Names: Nowell, Irene, 1940– author.
Title: Wisdom : the good life : wisdom literature and the rule of Benedict / Irene Nowell, OSB.
Description: Collegeville, Minnesota : Liturgical Press, 2017. | Includes bibliographical references.
Identifiers: LCCN 2016054421 (print) | LCCN 2017007336 (ebook) | ISBN 9780814645536 | ISBN 9780814645789 (ebook)
Subjects: LCSH: Wisdom literature—Criticism, interpretation, etc. | Benedict, Saint, Abbot of Monte Cassino. Regula. | Christian life—Catholic authors. | Spiritual life—Catholic Church. | Catholic Church—Doctrines.
Classification: LCC BS1455 .N69 2017 (print) | LCC BS1455 (ebook) | DDC 223—dc23
LC record available at https://lccn.loc.gov/2016054421

*In gratitude to my Sisters of Mount St. Scholastica
who give me examples of wisdom every day*

"The topic of wisdom is uniquely suited to Irene Nowell. She has lived for years under St. Benedict's Rule, which is a kind of Wisdom literature, as it insists that the holy is to be found in our everyday experiences and everyday encounters with other people. Nowell is also a Hebrew scholar and brings a treasure house of biblical knowledge to bear on the subject of what it means to be wise and to seek the wisdom that allows us to live a richer, more holy, and more loving life."

— Kathleen Norris, author of *Dakota* and *The Cloister Walk*

"Irene Nowell has drawn deep from the well of wisdom, sourced in Scripture and the Rule of Saint Benedict. She offers a set of simple yet profound reflections, points to consider, and prayers perfect for times and seasons of spiritual renewal and retreat."

— Sarah Schwartzberg, OSB
Editor, *Spirit & Life*

"Sister Irene here presents us with an introduction to Wisdom Literature in *Wisdom: The Good Life*. She skillfully weaves together themes from those texts that have so profoundly penetrated her life, the Sacred Scriptures and the Rule of St. Benedict, with the liturgy subtly threading through the entire work. A master teacher, she draws instruction from these works that can guide us through the ordinary but significant issues of daily life, helping us to find joy in the present moment and guiding us along the path to wisdom. Nowell has crafted a work that can both delight the general reader and open more profound insights for those who wish to ponder further."

— Abbot Placid Solari, OSB
Belmont Abbey

Contents

Foreword

Abbot John Klassen, OSB

Sister Irene Nowell is a distinguished scholar and teacher who has spent the last thirty-five years engaged in translation of the Old Testament Scriptures, as well as serving on the ICEL and NABRE translation committees for the Psalms and on the Committee on Illumination and Text for the Saint John's Bible. Through all of this she has been a living, listening, and praying member of a monastic community of Benedictine women in Atchison, Kansas.

This book is a work of synthesis and integration, of reflection and self-examination, and of prayer. Sister Irene draws on themes across the entire range of the Bible—the wisdom books, the prophetic literature, the Psalms, the Pentateuch—and weaves a garment that comes from having heard, read, studied, and reflected over a lifetime. It would be easy to isolate the wisdom tradition from the rest of the biblical tradition out of which it was born. Sister Irene does the opposite: she shows the multiple connections to the rest of the biblical tradition.

Sister Irene makes it clear why monastic life is called the wisdom tradition; both are inherently inductive, depending on and honoring lived experience. Sister Irene notes that "this reliance on experience makes the biblical wisdom literature the most incarnational literature in the Old Testament." Thus, when someone expresses an interest in monastic life, we may have a number of conversations with the individual, to discern the intensity of the interest. At that point, however, we say simply, "Come and see." Because it is an experiential, wisdom-based life, the seeker can't think her way into monastic life!

In posing the questions of what it means to live a "good life," why one would care to do so, and what the outcome is of that search, Sister Irene brings her repertoire of teaching skills to the task, drawing the reader into personal reflection—this is not going to be a "fly-over" engagement. She skillfully addresses the challenge of suffering in our world, the alternative proposals for wealth and security that have been proposed since human beings have been on the planet, and the importance of deep listening for gaining wisdom. "If you do not hear the cry of the poor, neither will you hear the voice of God who does hear their cry. There is no such thing as selective deafness."

Finally, her study and reflection as a Christian monastic woman lead to a consideration of how early Christian theologians such as Paul or the author of the letter to the Hebrews found in wisdom literature a set of images, texts, ideas, and reflections that were brilliantly suited to describe the person and work of Jesus Christ. Sister Irene notes that the Wisdom Woman becomes the strongest, most coherent, most poetically described image of God in the Old Testament. It is that image which Saint Paul and the author of the letter to the Hebrews absorb into their respective Christologies.

This book is intended to be chewed on, savored, read, and reread. Because it arises from a prayerful reading and reflection on the Scriptures, it is itself a book that will not yield its fruit to a once-over-lightly reading. A prayerful, reflective effort will, however, yield a rich harvest of insight and joy.

Preface
What Is Wisdom? Who Is Wisdom?

The first move we must make, as we begin to ponder the meaning of Wisdom in Scripture, must be to pray that God will grant it to us.

> Merciful God of my ancestors,
> with a word you created all things;
> in wisdom you made humankind
> to care for your creatures
> with holiness and justice
> to rule with upright heart.

> Give me Wisdom who sits by your throne;
> never forget I am your child,
> your servant born of your handmaid,
> frail, given little time,
> with limited grasp of your laws.
> Yet even someone perfect
> is nothing without the Wisdom
> that comes from you.

> With you is Wisdom;
> she knows your works,
> was there when you made the world.
> She sees what you judge as best,
> knows what is right in your commands.

Send her from heaven,
from your glorious throne,
to be my companion,
to teach me your will.

Her understanding is complete;
she guides me wisely
through all I must do,
and guards me with her clear light (Wis 9:1-11; ICEL).

This we ask through Christ, our Lord,
Your Wisdom incarnate.

Amen.

This prayer leads us to ask three critical questions: What is Wisdom? Who is wise? Who is this Wisdom who knows God's works and teaches us how to be wise? Wisdom is not an abstract quality or virtue. It does not exist in some rarefied sphere or in dictionaries or how-to books. In order to grasp the full meaning of wisdom we need to experience it "in the flesh." We need to turn to our own experience and ponder this question: Who is your example of wisdom? Who do you know who is wise? Think of someone specific, someone you know. This person can be someone living or dead, someone in your family or among your friends. What is it about this person that makes you think he or she is wise? How does this person live? What does he or she know? What does this person do; how does this person act? Qualities that often characterize wise persons include patience, humility, honesty, common sense, a sense of humor, the ability to cope with ambiguity, and the grace to listen attentively to others. The wise person is also able to be wrong and to be fully alive in this present moment. What are other qualities that you have observed in people you consider wise?

Now, having focused on a living, breathing example, we must consider a second question: How did this person get to be wise? Most of us weren't born wise, so how did this person gain wisdom? The answer to this question is not simple. There is a complex interweaving of elements in becoming wise. But, first of all, didn't your wise person become wise through experience? Isn't that why we often associate wisdom with older persons? They have had enough experience to understand life and relationships and the world in general. But we know that just living a long time (or a short time) isn't enough. An old education journal once said, "Have you had thirty years' experience or one year's experience thirty times?" Reflecting on and learning from our experience is an important necessity for becoming wise. Because this wisdom is gained through common human experience, it is available to every human being. This reliance on experience also makes the biblical wisdom literature the most incarnational literature in the Old Testament.

The author of the biblical book of Wisdom knows that common human experience is the route to wisdom. He says:

> I too am a mortal, the same as all the rest,
>   and a descendant of the first one formed of earth.
> And in my mother's womb I was molded into flesh
>   in a ten-month period—body and blood,
>   from the seed of a man, and the pleasure that
>   accompanies marriage.
> And I too, when born, inhaled the common air,
>   and fell upon the kindred earth;
>   wailing, I uttered that first sound common to all.
> In swaddling clothes and with constant care I was
>   nurtured.

For no king has any different origin or birth;
one is the entry into life for all,
and in one same way they leave it.
Therefore I prayed, and prudence was given me;
I pleaded and the spirit of Wisdom came to me.
(Wis 7:1-7)[1]

1. Common human experience is one principle. But there are more skills that must be learned in order to become wise. Your wise person probably also has a healthy relationship with God, a sense of reverence and awareness of God's loving presence in good times and bad. This wise person knows how to pray deeply and frequently. God is at the center of his or her reality. This person is also able and willing to be surprised by God, finding God in unexpected places and persons. These qualities are true whatever the person's religious affiliation is and however God is understood to be. We sometimes call this second principle fear of the Lord. 2

3. A third characteristic of a wise person is the capacity to enjoy life no matter what happens. Think again about your wise person. Isn't this someone who knows how to live well? Isn't that, in the end, what wisdom really is? The quality of knowing how to live well? Walter Brueggemann uses David as his model of wisdom. It's surprising, since Solomon is usually considered the patron saint of wisdom.[2] But Brueggemann's reason is this: David really lived. He says that you can accuse David of a lot of things, but you cannot accuse him of not having lived. There will always be sorrow and tragedy; the wise person knows how to grieve.

---

[1] All biblical quotations are from NABRE unless otherwise indicated.

[2] Walter Brueggemann, *In Man We Trust: The Neglected Side of Biblical Faith* (Atlanta: John Knox Press, 1972), see especially pp. 32–40.

As one of my wisest mentors said, "I may go to bed miserable every night; but I will wake up happy every morning." It takes courage to choose deep happiness even in the midst of suffering, but this courage is planted deep in those who are wise. Whatever does not lead to life is not wise, but, paradoxically, it takes wisdom to discern what leads to life.

These three characteristics are summarized in three principles of wisdom. The beginning of wisdom is fear of the Lord. The basis of wisdom is common human experience. The goal of wisdom is life, the good life. We will explore all three of them in detail. Now I suggest that you consider again your wise person. Ponder how this person got to be wise, what his or her wisdom looks like. Does this person know how to live well? What makes you think so? Does this person relate deeply to God? How do you know? What is God's gift to him or her? In the process, you may want to begin to ponder your own life. Are you wise? How did you get that way? What does wisdom look like? In the end, can you define wisdom?

We define and probe wisdom through our own human experience, but we are not dependent on our own resources alone. We have excellent examples of the wisdom of the ages. As we proceed we will consider five biblical books that heighten our understanding of wisdom: Proverbs, Job, Ecclesiastes (also known by its Hebrew name Qoheleth), Sirach (also known as the Wisdom of Ben Sira), and Wisdom. These books stretch over several centuries. The final form of the book of Proverbs, which is formed from several collections of pithy sayings, is considered to date from the sixth and fifth centuries BCE. The book of Job is difficult to date. The story of Job seems to be older than the poetry. The formation of the whole book is dated to the seventh to fifth centuries BCE. Ecclesiastes is believed to have been written in the third century BCE. Dating the book of Sirach is much easier. Ben Sira's grandson indicates the date of his translation of the book into Greek is around 117 BCE, so the writing of the original must be in the early second century BCE. Finally, the book of Wisdom, which was written in Greek, is commonly believed to have been written around 50 BCE. This "youngest" book is the only one of the five that expresses a belief in life after death. Thus the biblical wisdom books date from the seventh to the first centuries BCE, truly a gift to us as we probe this wisdom tradition.

Another source that is useful is the Rule of Benedict, which is itself a work of wisdom literature. Contemporary sources are also helpful. Finally, we have the experience of family, friends, and school. Wisdom is everywhere around us. We have only to tap into this wonderful flowing river (see Sir 24:25-33).

I intend to put this reflection on wisdom under the patronage of St. Scholastica, someone who is very wise. Scholastica's name comes from the root *schola* which means "leisure." So the ideas of contemplation and study flow from this root. Who knew when we were in "school" that it was a place of leisure! I'm not sure that our musical *schola* thinks our practices are all that leisurely either. But it is a gift of "leisure" to have the time for study and singing.

Monastics consider our life to be a "school of the Lord's service." Do we consider it to be a place of leisure? Not often, I suspect. Nonetheless, as hard as we work and as we will certainly continue to work, I do think monastic life is indeed intended to be a life of holy leisure—a life in which we can and do take time (prime time) to pray and to read, time to walk and to enjoy the beautiful world God has given us, time to be still and to hear the voice of God in our hearts. That is holy leisure. That is a way to cultivate wisdom.

So I invite you to enjoy some reflective time with this book, to enjoy the opportunity to practice holy leisure.

Spend this time with Scholastica (or your own wise and holy figure) and let her teach you that we don't always have to be rushing back to our responsibilities. What do holy people teach us about how to live well? Spend some time with God in your own heart and let God take care of you and the rest of the world. Finally, keep your wise person in view as you reach out to enjoy the goal of wisdom: the good life!

Consider

Do you have the courage to really live?

What stops you?

Who encourages you?

Prayer

Loving and generous God,
you who are the Giver of Life,
teach us to live our lives fully
trusting in your ever-present care.
This we ask in the name of Jesus,
who was and is always completely alive. Amen.

Fear of the Lord
Beginning of Wisdom

elden Lane says that an emotion the desert never fails to evoke is fear:

The emotion I felt . . . was not all that different from the emotion I felt upon being in extreme positions at other times in my life, whether it was pulling myself up a rope as a child, climbing a mountain as a teenager, or scuba diving as an adult: fear. Fear that I might lose control. Fear that I might fail. Fear that I might disappoint myself. When your god is self-reliance, and you let yourself down, there is nowhere else to turn.

This reaction, I was coming to see, is the first lesson of the desert: By feeling uneasy and unsure, by fearing that you're out of your depth and therefore might falter, by feeling small, and alone, you begin—slowly, reluctantly, maybe even for the first time in your life—to consider turning somewhere else. At first that somewhere else is some*one* else: a Moses, an

Aaron, an Avner [his guide]. But ultimately, maybe
even inevitably that some*one* else is some*thing* else.
For the secret lesson of remapping yourself, as I was
just finding, is that you eventually grow wary of the
flat and easy, the commonplace and self-reliant. You
begin to crave the depth, the height, the extremes. You
begin even to crave the fear.[1]

Proverbs tells us that fear of the Lord is the beginning
of wisdom (Prov 9:10; see also Ps 111:10). I would like to
begin the consideration of fear of the Lord by thinking a
little about who and what we are. One definition of fear of
the Lord is to know that God is God and I am not. As I've
gotten older, I've added a third phrase: God is God and I am
not and I am glad! But what does it mean that God is God
and I am not? We go back to creation. Wisdom tells us in
Proverbs 8 that she was there when God created the world,
there as God's designer, God's architect (Prov 8:22-30). So
she can tell us what we need to know about living the good
life. She can tell us who and what we are.

Now pondering our call to be fully human, to be living
images of God, certainly puts the fear of God in me. As
St. Benedict says, this is where we begin. In his invitation
to his followers, Benedict says, "If you hear God's voice
today, do not harden your hearts. . . . And again: you
that have ears to hear, listen to what the Spirit says to the
churches. . . . And what does he say? Come and listen to
me . . . ; I will teach you the fear of the Lord" (RB Prol.10-
12).[2] Fear of the Lord is the beginning of wisdom, as both

[1] Belden Lane, *Walking the Bible: A Journey by Land through the Five Books of Moses* (New York: HarperCollins, 2001), 223–24.
[2] *RB 1980: The Rule of St. Benedict* (Collegeville, MN: Liturgical Press, 1981), 159. All quotations from the Rule of Benedict are taken from this translation.

Proverbs and the Psalms teach us (Prov 1:7; Ps 111:10), so if we are going to live this good life, this wisdom life, if we are going to be fully human, we must embrace fear of the Lord.

Sometimes we do not like this phrase, "fear of the Lord," because it suggests to us that we should be afraid of God. That mistaken idea, however, occurs because the meaning of "fear" in the English language has shrunk, not because "fear of the Lord" is a scary thing. So we need to go back to the source, Scripture, to draw out the full meaning of the phrase, "fear of the Lord."

What really is fear of the Lord? A novice, who had been assigned to give a report on fear of the Lord, defined it this way, "Oh, my God!" (Say that phrase a few times as an exclamation of wonder.) The novice gives us the short answer. Sirach, who is really excited about fear of the Lord, gives us the long answer:

> The fear of the Lord is glory and exultation,
>   gladness and a festive crown.
> The fear of the Lord rejoices the heart,
>   giving gladness, joy, and long life.
> Those who fear the Lord will be happy at the end,
>   even on the day of death they will be blessed.
>
> The beginning of wisdom is to fear the Lord;
>   she is created with the faithful in the womb.
> With the godly she was created from of old,
>   and with their descendants she will keep faith.
>
> The fullness of wisdom is to fear the Lord;
>   she inebriates them with her fruits.
> Their entire house she fills with choice foods,
>   their granaries with her produce.
>
> The crown of wisdom is the fear of the Lord,
>   flowering with peace and perfect health.
> Knowledge and full understanding she rains down;
>   she heightens the glory of those who possess her.

The root of wisdom is to fear the Lord;
   her branches are long life.

If you desire wisdom, keep the commandments,
   and the Lord will bestow her upon you;
For the fear of the Lord is wisdom and discipline;
   faithfulness and humility are his delight.
      (Sir 1:11-20, 26-27)

The most compelling insight about fear of the Lord, however, comes from Psalm 130. In that psalm we begin by crying to God "out of the depths." We know that, if God is keeping track of our sins—if there really is a bank of file cabinets or a huge computer system in heaven—we are in deep trouble! But in verse 4 comes the amazing news: "with you is found forgiveness and so we fear you."[3] We fear God, not because God will be angry and punish our sins, but precisely because God forgives us! God's forgiveness is more than we can bear.

It is no wonder we say, "Oh, my God!" Fear of the Lord is awe at God's unfailing goodness; it is wonder at the beauty and intricacy of the world God created. It is love too great for our hearts to contain and terror that we might foolishly wound or separate ourselves from that love. It is everything to which we exclaim, "Oh, my God!"

So what does fear of the Lord look like in real life? How do people act who fear the Lord? What do the psalms tell us? "You who fear the LORD, trust in the LORD: your help and your shield is God" (Ps 115:11). With confidence they cry to God to save them from danger (Ps 145:19). Their confidence is not misplaced; God does save them: the angel of

---

[3] Translation mine. *Ecumenical Grail* translates, "that you may be revered," but I prefer to translate the Hebrew verb *yr'* with its common meaning, "fear."

the Lord encamps with them and rescues them (see Ps 34:8). "God will show them the path to choose" (Ps 25:12), will give food to them and satisfy their desires (see Ps 145:19). Nothing is lacking to those who fear God (see Ps 34:10). Those who fear the Lord love the Lord and "take great delight in God's commands" (Ps 112:1). Over and over we are told that they are happy (often translated "blessed"; Ps 112:1; 128:1). Fear of the Lord truly does warm the heart, as Sirach says.

The people who fear the Lord are those who have learned wisdom. Again and again Scripture tells us that "fear of the Lord is the beginning of wisdom" (Ps 111:10; see Sir 1:14). Even that is not enough for Sirach, however, who adds that fear of the Lord is also wisdom's fullness, crown, and root (Sir 1:16, 18, 20). So to really understand fear of the Lord we need to probe wisdom as thoroughly as we can. We want to know how to live well.

We have been thinking about wisdom all along. How has our understanding of wisdom deepened? Think again of the people you know who are wise. These are the people who show us what fear of the Lord is in the flesh, since fear of the Lord is wisdom's beginning, root, crown, and fruit. Are these not the people who throughout a lifetime are still capable of wonder and awe and love, who can be surprised every day? Aren't these the folks who are happy, who trust in God to get them out of difficulty and who delight in what God gives them? Aren't they our truly holy people?

St. Benedict wants his followers to learn fear of the Lord right at the beginning of the monastic journey: "Come and listen to me, . . . I will teach you the fear of the Lord" (RB Prol.12; see Ps 34:12). But Benedict does not tell us that fear of the Lord is the beginning of wisdom. Instead he tells us that it is the beginning of humility (RB 7.10). After a long meditation on all the steps of humility Benedict finally reveals where this fear of the Lord leads: "Now, therefore, after ascending all these steps of humility, we will quickly arrive at that perfect love of God which casts out fear" (RB 7.67). Here, Benedict tells us the good news: we begin to act "no longer out of fear of hell, but out of love for Christ, good habit, and delight in virtue" (RB 7.69). The perfect love of God does not cast out fear of the Lord but fear of hell. "Delight" is a major clue here. This is the delight that is characteristic of wisdom, characteristic of fear of the Lord. This is the delight children know, the capability to be totally captured by wonder at any moment in life. Isaiah says that the shoot that comes from the stump of Jesse will delight in fear of the Lord (see Isa 11:1-3). So in the Christian interpretation of that verse we find our "delight" in imitation of Christ, the shoot from the son of Jesse. Our delight is a sign of our love for him. This perfect love of Christ is, in fact, the fullness of fear of the Lord, the fullness of wisdom.

I learned the link between fear of the Lord and love from another novice! She pointed out that Proverbs 1:7 says that "fear of the Lord is the beginning of *knowledge*." So, it must be true that to fear God is to grow in knowledge of God. But the more we know God, the more we are filled with the love of God. The more we love God, the more we are awed by God, the more we fear God. So this movement becomes an ever-deepening spiral: to fear God is to know God; to know God is to love God more; to love God more is to fear God more. The ever-deepening spiral leads to the perfect love of God, as Benedict also teaches us.

The goal of wisdom is the good life. Scripture tells us that the way to that good life begins with fear of the Lord, that spirit of openness and wonder that is ready to say at any moment, "Oh, my God!" Happy are they who fear the Lord. All the days of their life they will be richly blessed (see Ps 128).

Consider

> When have you experienced awe and wonder at the
> awareness of God?
>
> What insights did you gain from that experience?

Prayer

> Gracious God,
> form us in the likeness of your Son
> and deepen his life within us.
> Teach us to live as witnesses of gospel joy
> in a world of fragile peace and broken promises.
> Touch the hearts of all people with your love
> that we in turn may learn to love one another.
> We ask this through Christ, your Wisdom and your
> Word.

Why Do Bad Things Happen to Good People?

The Mystery of Suffering

In Psalm 31 we pray:

> Have mercy on me, O Lord,
> for I am in distress.
> My eyes are wasted away with grief,
> as are my soul and my body.

> For my life is spent with sorrow,
> and my years with sighs.
> Affliction has broken down my strength,
> and my bones waste away. (Ps 31:10-11)[1]

To choose life; to live every day; to eat from the tree in the middle of the garden; to be human is to know good

---

[1] Unless otherwise indicated, all psalm quotations are from the *Ecumenical Grail Psalter* (Chicago: GIA Publications, 2015).

and bad. We have known loved ones who suffered from cancer or heart disease; we have seen the effects of terrible accidents. We have grieved over loved ones who have died; we sometimes wonder about the circumstances of our own death. Even Christ, according to the Letter to the Hebrews, "learned obedience from what he suffered" (Heb 5:8). Suffering, especially the suffering of good people, is a mystery, a problem for all of us from ancient Israel even until now. Suffering is one of the problems that the ancient wisdom writers pondered. They don't have any better answers than we do, but they do have some wisdom for us to ponder as we endure inevitable suffering.

Our first difficulty is the suspicion that suffering is punishment. We ask the age-old question: "What did I do to deserve this?" The answer is most likely "Nothing!" We think we know how the world should be. The good are supposed to be rewarded and the wicked punished. This theory, called the theory of retribution, seems as old as humankind. Deuteronomy expresses it clearly with a whole set of blessings for the people who obey God and a matching set of curses for those who disobey (see Deut 28). The history of Israel that follows in the books from Joshua to Kings illustrates the theory with example after example.

There is, after all, a kernel of truth in this theory. Sometimes suffering is my own fault. The problem for us is this doesn't always work! Too often for our liking the wicked get away with it. We complain in the words of Psalm 73:

> As for me, my feet came close to stumbling;
> my steps had almost slipped,
> for I was filled with envy of the proud,
> when I saw how the wicked prosper.
>
> For them there are no pains;
> their bodies are sound and sleek.

> They do not share in people's burdens;
> they are not stricken like others.
>
> So they wear their pride like a necklace;
> they clothe themselves with violence. (Ps 73:2-6)

In spite of the prosperity of the wicked, however, the insight remains true: sin does cause suffering. The theory just doesn't work on a one-to-one basis. All too often the sinner isn't the one who suffers, or at least isn't the only one. The absent parent doesn't pay child support and the child suffers. One generation destroys the ozone layer and the next generation suffers. Leaders of nations begin a war and the common people suffer. In fact, because we are the bridge to the rest of creation and have been given responsibility for the rest of creation, when we sin all creation suffers (see Gen 3:17-19; 6:7; 7:4).

Jeremiah even threatens to take God to court over this! He basically says, "If I lay charges against you, O Lord, I will be right, but you will win. Why must the land suffer for the wickedness of those who live on it" (see Jer 12:1-4). Jeremiah's problem really is ours. Why do the wicked prosper? Why do the good suffer? The psalmist goes on in Psalm 73:

> How useless to keep my heart pure,
> and wash my hands in innocence,
> when I was stricken all day long,
> suffered punishment with each new morning. (Ps 73:13-14)

This is the heart of Job's struggle. He is convinced that he has not sinned, that he does not deserve suffering. Therefore, if his suffering is not his fault, it must be God's!

> Know then that it is God who has dealt unfairly with me,
> and compassed me round with his net.
> Pity me, pity me, you my friends,
> for the hand of God has struck me! (Job 19:6, 21)

But Job's greatest anguish is that he does not understand. It is our greatest anguish too. "Why? Why me, O God!" The theory of retribution doesn't work. Sometimes the wicked suffer and the good prosper; sometimes the good suffer and the wicked prosper.

Christians, with the benefit of Jesus' example and the belief in life after death, have made some new attempts at understanding. One attempt is to reverse the theory. Perhaps it's true that the good suffer and the wicked prosper. If you suffer, you must be holy; if you're fat, dumb, and happy, you must be wicked! After all, Jesus suffered. But this doesn't work either. Whether you are good or wicked, it is inevitable that you will suffer, and sometimes the rich really are holy!

We Christians have an added temptation. We have bought the theory completely but we have just postponed it. If you're good, you will be rewarded in heaven; if you're wicked, you will be punished in hell—or at least in purgatory. But even in this, we can't hold God to our standards. Heaven is not a reward for what we have done or for how much we have suffered; heaven is a gift. We can never deserve it. In spite of all the attempts of the wisdom writers and of theologians throughout the millennia, in the end we have to stand with Job and admit that we really do not understand the mystery of suffering.

Perhaps we will finally have to admit that suffering is not punishment but simply a part of common human experience, that to eat from the tree of knowledge is to know good and bad. So, since we cannot fully understand the mystery of suffering and none of us can avoid suffering forever, we need to ask another question: what can suffering teach us?

First of all, suffering itself is never good; it is always absurd, always meaningless in and of itself. Suffering itself is not holy, even though what we do with it may be. Suffering is never to be sought for its own sake. That is masochism and in itself is sinful. The goal of wisdom is always life, the good life. If what we are doing is not directed toward life, it is not wisdom. It is not holy.

Nonetheless, none of us can avoid suffering, and some-times we choose to suffer for a good reason—for the sake of others, for better health down the road, for whatever. And sometimes suffering just comes. So what can we do with it? First of all, we can deny it: "Of course it doesn't hurt!" But the denial of suffering is the denial of reality, the denial of experience, and, as we already know, wisdom comes through experience. The way to the good life comes, paradoxically, through common human experience. Even though Job asked God to wipe the day of his birth off the calendar (Job 3:3-6), the days of pain exist right there along with the days of joy, and we are better off to face them. Otherwise our wisdom will be diminished. Otherwise we will know only half of what that tree teaches us—the knowl-edge of good and bad. Then we run the risk of not knowing the other half either! A second response we can make to suffering is the opposite. We can wallow in it. We've all been tempted sometimes to try this. But this too is a denial of experience and a denial of hope, a refusal or an inability to accept God's wisdom and to trust in God's care for us.

So, neither denying suffering nor wallowing in it is the solution. How else can we respond? There is a third option. We can live our way through suffering, always choosing life. As St. Benedict says in his description of humility: "[Our] heart quietly embraces suffering and endures it without weakening or seeking escape" (RB 7.35-36). Paul gives us good advice too: "Rejoice in hope, endure in affliction, per-severe in prayer" (Rom 12:12). My favorite piece of advice is in the First Letter of Peter: "Always be ready to give an explanation to anyone who asks you for a reason for your hope" (1 Pet 3:15). Many of us have had that good example with our own family members or friends.

How can we learn to embrace hope in the midst of pain? It seems that the real key to living our way through suffering is in the relationships that are at the heart of wisdom: the relationship with God and with each other. We do not have to do this alone, and we do not have to suffer in silence. We do everything we can to ease each other's pain, and sometimes the best thing we can do is what Job's friends did for the first seven days: sit with the sufferer in silence (see Job 2:12-13).

The relationship with God is, in the end, what strengthens us to endure suffering. Scripture indicates that the proper response in any trouble is to cry out to God. When the Israelites are suffering in Egypt, it is only when they cry out to God that God summons Moses to set the exodus event in motion (see Exod 2:23-25). Throughout the book of Judges, it is when the people cry out that God sends a judge to deliver them from their oppressors and relieve their pain (see, e.g., Judg 3:9, 15; 4:3; 6:6-7). In Psalm 88, the psalmist keeps reminding God, "I cry before you day and night" (Ps 88:2). We have lots of lament psalms and we need them most when we are suffering. The biblical message is: "Cry early and often!"

That's what Job is doing. For almost thirty chapters Job cries out to God, and his crying out is not nice. Job says terrible things to God, accuses God of injustice and vindictiveness or of plain inattention. Yet at the end of the book, God says that Job is the one who speaks rightly. The friends, who have valiantly defended God throughout, will only be *forgiven* for what they have said if Job prays for them (Job 42:7-9)! How can this be? The difference is that Job speaks *to* God; the friends only talk *about* God. Job will not deny his own reality, but neither will he let go of God. At the end of his laments he challenges God: "here is my signature: let the Almighty answer me!" (Job 31:35).

Job is in good company. Moses complains to God all the way across the desert—forty years' worth (see, e.g., Num 11:10-15). (Notice: it's all right to complain to God; complaining to each other is the problem!) Jeremiah too says, "You seduced me, LORD, and I let myself be seduced" (Jer 20:7). The psalmist of Psalm 88 won't let go of God either:

> *You* have laid me in the depths of the pit,
> in regions that are dark and deep.
> *Your* anger weighs down upon me;
> I am drowned beneath *your* waves.
> *You* have taken away my friends;
> to them *you* have made me hateful. (Ps 88:7-9, italics mine)

Finally the psalmist cries out, "Why do you reject me, O LORD" (Ps 88:14). This psalm does not take God off the hook at the end. Now it is God's move. God has to do something.

Throughout the biblical laments, however, this crying out to God is balanced by an awareness and acceptance of the freedom of God. Even in his most terrible pain, Job keeps saying that God is free to act according to divine wisdom: "Who can say to him, 'What are you doing?'" (Job 9:12b). Qoheleth, in a somber mood, says: "Consider the work of God. Who can make straight what God has made crooked? On a good day enjoy good things, and on an evil day consider: Both the one and the other God has made, so that no one may find the least fault with him" (Eccl 7:13-14).

The sage's advice is to accept life every day, enjoy the good when you have it, accept suffering when it comes. He says,

> Sorrow is better than laughter;
>   when the face is sad, the heart grows wise.
> The heart of the wise is in the house of mourning,
>   but the heart of fools is in the house of merriment.
>   (Eccl 7:3-4)

Or as a modern proverb puts it: "Sorrow with his pick mines the heart, making channels for joy to enter when he is gone."

But Qoheleth is not a sad sack. Far from it! He keeps affirming life: "A live dog is better off than a dead lion!" (Eccl 9:4; see also Eccl 5:17-19). The life God gives us, with all its joy and sorrow, is a gift. In the end, like Job, we do not understand. But it is the relationship that remains. God comes to talk to Job at the end of the book. With a series of questions, God draws Job into God's own experience:

> Where were you when I founded the earth?
>   Tell me, if you have understanding. . . .
> Do you know when mountain goats are born,
>   or watch for the birth pangs of deer? . . .
> Does the eagle fly up at your command
>   to build his nest up high? (Job 38:4; 39:1, 27)

For Job this experience of God's presence is enough. Even before God takes away his suffering he accepts his lack of understanding and accepts God's freedom:

> I know that you can do all things,
>   and that no purpose of yours can be hindered. . . .
> I have spoken but did not understand,
>   things too marvelous for me, which I did not know. . . .
> By hearsay I had heard of you,
>   but now my eye has seen you. (Job 42:2, 3b-c, 5)

It is the relationship with God that makes the difference, not the relief from pain.

The psalmist of Psalm 73 comes to the same acceptance:

> I was stupid and did not understand;
> I was like a beast in your sight.
>
> As for me, I was always in your presence;
> you were holding me by my right hand.

By your counsel you will guide me,
and then you will lead me to glory.

What else have I in heaven but you?
Apart from you, I want nothing on earth.
My flesh and my heart waste away;
God is the strength of my heart,
my portion forever. . . .

For me to be near God is good;
I have made the Lord GOD my refuge.
I will proclaim your works
at the gates of daughter Zion. (Ps 73:22-26, 28)

What is vital is the relationship. Our relationship with
God is a real relationship, not a cringing submission. When
suffering strikes, we cry out like hell! We complain to God;
we bargain with God; we accuse God; we say terrible things.
And if we don't have the courage or the imagination to
say our own terrible things to God, the psalms, which are
God's own word, give us plenty of material. But even as
we cry out, we also give God the freedom to do whatever
is in God's wisdom to do. We don't understand it—and we
complain about that too—but because we love God and
because we trust that God loves us, even when it seems
utterly stupid to trust, we accept our human nature. We
agree to be fully human.

In the end it is the relationship that saves us. Throughout
almost the whole Old Testament there is no real belief in
life after death. Only in very late Old Testament times does
the idea of immortality emerge. Our belief in resurrection is
a Christian idea. How could we have understood it before
Christ? But one of the late wisdom writers got a glimmer.
It all has to do with relationship. The writer of the book of
Wisdom (about 50 BCE) first takes God off the hook: "God
did not make death, nor does [God] rejoice in the destruc-

tion of the living" (Wis 1:13). So where does death come from? This sage says, "It was the wicked who with hands and words invited death, / considered it a friend and pined for it / and made a covenant with it" (Wis 1:16). Death, eternal death, is not a punishment but a choice. The wicked made a covenant with death rather than a covenant with God. So, the wisdom writer observes, it is righteousness that is undying (Wis 1:15).

Righteousness is based always on the demands of the relationship. So, if righteousness is undying, and righteousness is the relationship between us and God, then we will not die. We cannot die! If we die, the relationship is broken, but the relationship is undying! The news here is: we will live forever, not because of our own nature, not even because we are so wonderful, but because of our relationship with God. God simply cannot let go of us! And we had better not let go of God!

Finally we know the truth: suffering is real, but it is not the end. Not even death is the end, because our relationship with God cannot die. We, created in the image of God and breathing with the breath of God, cannot simply cease to exist. This turns the whole question of suffering on its head. The writer of Wisdom goes on:

> The souls of the righteous are in the hand of God,
>   and no torment shall touch them.
> They seemed, in the view of the foolish, to be dead;
>   and their passing away was thought an affliction
>   and their going forth from us, utter destruction.
> But they are in peace.
> For if to others, indeed, they seem punished,
>   yet is their hope full of immortality;
> Chastised a little, they shall be greatly blessed,
>   because God tried them
>   and found them worthy of himself.

As gold in the furnace, he proved them,
    and as sacrificial offerings he took them to himself. . . .
Those who trust in him shall understand truth,
    and the faithful shall abide with him in love:
Because grace and mercy are with his holy ones,
    and his care is with the elect. (Wis 3:1-6, 9)

The relationship with God is undying. It is this relationship that saves us. The amazing mystery is this: in the fullness of time, when God, the Wisdom of God, chose to become incarnate, God's wisdom did not eliminate human suffering but rather chose to share it. Our suffering is not gone because of Christ, but it is no longer meaningless. Christ, being willing to be fully human, also accepted the final human weakness, even death (see Phil 2:6-8). He too "learned obedience [i.e., wisdom] from what he suffered" (Heb 5:8). He has shown us the way to live through suffering into life. He recognized and acknowledged the reality of his suffering. He said, "My soul is sorrowful even to death" (Matt 26:38; Mark 14:34). He cried out in anguish to his Father, "take this cup away from me" (Luke 22:42). But he also accepted the freedom and the wisdom of God: "Not my will, but yours be done" (Luke 22:42). Through his wounds we are healed (see 1 Pet 2:24).

This is why Paul can say,

I consider that the sufferings of this present time are as nothing compared with the glory to be revealed for us. For creation awaits with eager expectation the revelation of the children of God. . . . [C]reation itself [will] be set free from slavery to corruption and share in the glorious freedom of the children of God. We know that all creation is groaning in labor pains even until now; and not only that, but we ourselves, who have the firstfruits of the Spirit [that breath by

which we breathe], we also groan within ourselves as
we wait for adoption, the redemption of our bodies.
(Rom 8:18-19, 21-23)

Our redemption, our life, our hope, is in the undying relationship with God.

What will separate us from the love of Christ? Will anguish, or distress, or persecution, or famine, or naked-
ness, or peril, or the sword? As it is written: / "For your
sake we are being slain all the day; / we are looked
upon as sheep to be slaughtered." / No, in all these
things we conquer overwhelmingly through him who
loved us. For I am convinced that neither death, nor
life, nor angels, nor principalities, nor present things,
nor future things, nor powers, nor height, nor depth,
nor any other creature will be able to separate us from
the love of God in Christ Jesus our Lord. (Rom 8:35-39)

In all these things we conquer overwhelmingly through the
one who has so greatly loved us! This is indeed the good life!

Consider

Who do you know who is suffering?

How can you support him or her?

Prayer

Compassionate God,
you who grieve with us,
whose heart is broken by our pain,
touch us in your love
that we may be strengthened and consoled.
This we ask in the name of Jesus
by whose wounds we are healed.

Wisdom and Creation

Most of the biblical reflection on creation outside of Genesis is found in the wisdom literature. In Proverbs 8 Wisdom tells us:

The LORD begot me, the beginning of his works,
  the forerunner of his deeds of long ago;
From of old I was formed,
  at the first, before the earth.
When there were no deeps I was brought forth,
  when there were no fountains or springs of water;
Before the mountains were settled into place,
  before the hills, I was brought forth;
When the earth and the fields were not yet made,
  nor the first clods of the world.
When he established the heavens, there was I,
  when he marked out the vault over the face of the deep;
When he made firm the skies above,
  when he fixed fast the springs of the deep;
When he set for the sea its limit,
  so that the waters should not transgress his command;
When he fixed the foundations of earth,
  then was I beside him as artisan [Heb. ʿamon];

I was his delight day by day,
   playing before him all the while,
Playing over the whole of his earth,
   having my delight with human beings. (Prov 8:22-31)

Wisdom has an intimate relationship with creation; she was there from the beginning. She was the designer at God's right hand. So we know that Wisdom can tell us how to live well. She can tell us who and what we are.

We must begin, however, with Genesis, which gives us two stories of creation: the very formal, beautifully structured story of Genesis 1:1–2:4a, and the homey, heartwarming story of Genesis 2:4b-25. (There seems to have been an editorial principle throughout Scripture: Don't throw anything away!) Each story has something to say to us about who and what we are; each story has its own wisdom.

Arthur Miller says that "the greatness of [Genesis 1] lies in its infinite suggestiveness. It is full of thisness and thatness and very little whyness, and so it tends to keep its reader awake and perhaps a little more alive."[1] So what is the "thisness and thatness" that we can learn from Genesis 1? This story tells us that God created human beings, male and female, in the divine image. We all know this; you can probably recite the text by heart. But how many of us believe it? How many mornings do you get up and thank God for being created in God's image? How many nights do you go to bed and wonder if you really are in God's image? Perhaps we need to retool our imaginations, our ability to image God. Perhaps we need to learn to believe the Word of God that tells us that we are indeed in God's image.

---

[1] Arthur Miller, "The Story of Adam and Eve," in *Genesis as It Is Written*, ed. David Rosenberg (San Francisco: HarperSanFrancisco, 1996), 41.

In ancient Israel's interpretation of the Ten Commandments, the saying that one should not make any image or
"likeness of anything" was interpreted quite strictly (see
Exod 20:4-6). Thus the only image of God the people were
allowed was each other. This restriction actually is a great
gift. Even though we Christians have crucifixes and statues
and paintings of Jesus, this reality is still true for us too: the
best image of God you have is the person sitting next to you
or the next person you meet/As Christians the way we most
frequently touch the Body of Christ is in every human being
we touch. When you get up tomorrow morning and look in
the mirror (or perhaps you should wait till after breakfast),
you should be awed at the realization that you yourself are
a living, breathing image of God-in-the-flesh. /

The Genesis text continues with God's blessing of
humankind. Blessing is always a sharing in God's life and
power. God says: "Be fertile and multiply; fill the earth
and subdue it" (Gen 1:28). God gives us human beings the
power to continue creation—in all the ways that we are
"creative"—and God also gives us responsibility: fill the
earth and "subdue" it or "have dominion" over it. My best
analogy for this situation is that God is like a parent who
leaves home and puts the oldest child in charge: "Take care
of your brothers and sisters and the house." The parent does
not intend that the oldest child now has absolute power
to trash the house and lock the younger children in the
closet. The parent entrusts the child with the responsibility
of caring for things and people as the parent would do.
Being created in the image of God gives us the responsibility
of acting like God and caring for each other and the rest
of the world as God would do. Psalm 8, a meditation on
Genesis 1, demonstrates this with a wonderful verse right in
the center:

What are human beings that you are mindful of them
 . . . ?
You have made them little less than a god,
   crowned them with glory and honor,
given them rule over the works of your hands. (Ps 8:5-7;
   my translation)

But, as Walter Brueggemann points out,[2] Psalm 8 only works because we have God holding everything together at both beginning and end: "O LORD, our Lord, / how awesome is your name through all the earth" (Ps 8:2, 10). If we are not surrounded by God at all times we get ourselves and the rest of creation in deep trouble!

God's final word on all this—on having created us in the divine image, shared creative power with us, and entrusted us with responsibility of caring for everything else—is delighted approval! God's final word is "How good! How very good!" (see Gen 1:4, 10, 12, 18, 21, 25, 31). One morning as I was doing *lectio* I had a great insight regarding this response of God to creating us. I was reading Psalm 100 and realized that in that psalm (and several others) we, who have been proclaimed good by God in Genesis 1, now look back at God and say in turn: "How good!" (Ps 100:5; Hebrew *ki tob*). It seems we have a mutual admiration society, we and God each declaring that the other is very good!

Thus Scripture tells us that the more we are what we are created to be, the more we will be like God. The more human we are, the more we will be like God; the more we are like God the more human we will be. Have you ever said, "Oh, yes. I really made a mess of that; I'm only human"? This

---

[2] Walter Brueggemann, *The Message of the Psalms* (Minneapolis: Augsburg, 1984), 37–38.

"only human" is the best image of God we have. Perhaps we need to think more about what it means to be human, what it means to be images of God. Does it mean to be "perfect"? Are the perfectionists among us really on the right track? This leads us to the second story: Genesis 2–3.

In Genesis 2 we find the Lord God down on the divine knees, forming a human creature out of the clay of the ground. After forming the creature, God blows into its nostrils the breath of life, and so the clay creature becomes a living human being. What is this story saying about who and what we are? We are lovingly formed by God the potter, whose fingerprints are still on us. Poets always understand these things better than we do. Mary Lou Sleevi takes a little poetic license in imagining God's creation of Eve:

> Eve comes alive, dripping wet, from God's fingers,
> Capstone of Creation in clay.
> Unique,
> Herself.
> She was the final touch from the hand of the Potter,
> Whose fingerprints were impressed in her forever.[3]

Imagine feeling God's fingerprints on you, in you! Imagine seeing God's fingerprints on your brothers and sisters. I have a good friend who is a potter. I love what she makes because it brings her presence, her fingerprints, to me. What does that mean for us who are marked by God's fingerprints? We are formed by God; we live by the breath God blew into us, by the spirit of God. We belong to both heaven and earth. We are one with the rest of creation, formed out of the clay of the ground, but we live by the breath of God. We have become the bridge between God and the rest of

---

[3] Mary Lou Sleevi, *Women of the Word* (Notre Dame, IN: Ave Maria Press, 1989), 15.

creation. We are, if you will, the lungs for the rest of the world! If we separate from God, we cut off our air supply, but the rest of creation then suffocates with us. The prophets tell us that over and over: "How long must the land mourn . . . because of the wickedness of those who dwell in it" (Jer 12:4)?

Human beings are indeed wonderful, but life in the garden does not go on happily ever after. There is a matter of two trees and a snake. In the center of the garden God planted the tree of life and the tree of the knowledge of good and bad. These trees are a bit mysterious. After this verse, they never appear together again. Some of the early Christian writers wondered if they were actually the same tree—and I wonder the same thing. They are clearly both wisdom trees. Wisdom herself is identified as the tree of life in Proverbs (Prov 3:18) and the goal of wisdom is the good life. So if we keep eating of the banquet that Wisdom provides, we will indeed live.

The other tree, the tree of the knowledge of good and bad, is the tree of experience. In Hebrew "to know" connotes having and learning from experience. The basis of wisdom is common human experience, so, in a way, we eat from this second tree daily also. It is important to remember that this tree gives the knowledge of *both* good and bad. We usually remember just the bad, but the story suggests that unless they eat of this tree, they will know *neither* good *nor* bad. Life in the garden is not yet the good life; it is still a life without the richness of experience. The Hebrew idiom "to know good and bad" means to be mature, in fact, to be wise. St. Irenaeus observes that the two in the garden are very young, perhaps adolescents (see *Adversus Haeresus* 4.38.1).

So what is the problem here? Why can't they eat of this tree? Before we can answer that question we have to deal with the snake. After trying to drive a wedge of suspicion between God and the human beings—that mean old God won't let you eat any of this wonderful fruit—the serpent comes to the real point: "If you eat of this tree you will be like God." Well! If we remember Genesis 1 (and if we read the Genesis chapters in order), they already *are* like God. So the desire to be like God is not the problem; it is actually the *right* desire. To be like God is to be what God created them (and us) to be! So that is not the problem. The problem lies in how they (and we) go about trying to be like God. The serpent suggests that the way to be like God is to turn against God, to mistrust God's motives, to disobey God's commands, to take charge. The serpent's message is: "Obviously God doesn't want you to be in the divine likeness. Otherwise God would have *commanded* you to eat from the fruit of this tree. But God is keeping you from it. So you'd better do something about it yourselves. You can't trust God to keep creating you in the divine image. Depend on no one but yourselves!"

Well, we know how well that worked! They ate from the tree and, sure enough, they discovered the difference between good and bad. Isn't this always the way? The first experience they discovered was bad. So this brilliant Genesis writer describes for us the consequences of sin: alienation, separation, mistrust. They separate from each other, first with clothes—we don't wear them only to keep warm—and then by blaming. They separate from God by hiding and again blaming. Adam says, "It's not my fault. The woman *you* put here gave me the fruit. It's her fault and yours." They also separate from the rest of creation—they who are supposed to be responsible for it—by blaming the serpent, and with him the rest of the animal kingdom. The earth itself is cursed because of them; they have cut off the air supply, the breath of God. Finally access to the tree of life, the other tree, is barred. This is certainly not the good life!

St. Irenaeus says that the problem with the two in the garden is not that they wanted to be like God but that they wanted to be like God without being willing *to be human*![4] In other words, they did not want to be *like* God; they wanted to *be* God. Bad idea! They wanted to be perfect. They were not willing to learn from their mistakes, to be wrong, to be humiliated by weakness, to know good and bad through living, through experience. They wanted instant knowledge like instant coffee—no time to let it percolate through life. They did not believe that they really were images of God. They thought God hadn't created them well enough, that they had to improve on the original. Surely this weak, fallible, bumbling human nature couldn't be the image of God. This certainly could not be the best God could do! There must be a better way.

But there isn't a better way! God, more amazing than we can ever imagine, has created us in the divine image. The best image that God knows how to create is this weak, fallible, bumbling human nature. "The foolishness of God is wiser than human wisdom!" (1 Cor 1:25). We have a hard time looking at ourselves as God sees us. We don't always believe the words Psalm 139 puts in our mouths: "I thank you who wonderfully made me" (Ps 139:14). We keep trying to remake the image, keep trying to improve on God's design. We keep trying to be "perfect." We want to be like God without being willing to be human.

Kilian McDonnell has an insightful poem titled "Perfection, Perfection":

> I have had it with perfection.
> I have packed my bags,

---

[4] Aelred Squire, *Asking the Fathers: The Art of Inspiration and Prayer* (Ramsey, NJ: Paulist Press, 1973), 24–25.

I am out of here.
Gone.

As certain as rain
will make you wet,
perfection will do you
in.

It droppeth not as dew
upon the summer grass
to give liberty and green
joy.

Perfection straineth out
the quality of mercy,
withers rapture at its
birth.

Before the battle is half begun,
cold probity thinks
it can't be won, concedes the
war.

I've handed in my notice,
given back my keys,
signed my severance check, I
quit.

Hints I could have taken:
Even the perfect chiseled form of
Michelangelo's radiant David
squints.

The Venus de Milo
has no arms,
the Liberty Bell is
cracked.[5]

---

[5] Kilian McDonnell, *Swift, Lord, You Are Not* (Collegeville, MN: Saint John's University Press, 2003), 34–35.

Where does this leave us? We human beings are created in the image of God, blessed with God's creative power and entrusted with responsibility for the rest of creation. We are clay of the earth, breathing with the breath of God. We are the bridge between God and the rest of creation; we breathe God's spirit on the rest of creation. We bring all creation to God in our prayer. All this is true of each of us, male and female—every human being. The right desire is the desire to be like God. For us that desire is indeed holiness, is indeed wisdom. But the way we go about being like God is crucial. The way to be like God is to learn to be as fully human as we can be. We have a hard time believing that this is the way to the good life, but, in fact, it is the only way. We are called to live day after day, finding God in every experience of life whether good or bad. The Genesis text seems to suggest that God intended all along to give us the knowledge of good and bad but that God knew we could only digest this fruit slowly, throughout a lifetime. The goal of wisdom is life, to live ourselves into fuller and fuller images of God through all the years God gives us. This is where the trees really do become one: the tree of the knowledge of good and bad is the tree of life.

We are not left to discover this on our own, however. We have a living example, the human being fully alive that Irenaeus describes. Jesus is God's best way of teaching us how to be like God, of teaching us how to be fully human, of showing us the good life. Jesus is fully human. The Letter to the Hebrews says he is like us, "tested in every way, yet without sin" (Heb 4:15). Not only is Jesus fully human, but, unlike the two in the garden, he is *willing* to be human. The Letter to the Philippians confirms this:

> Christ Jesus, . . .
> though he was in the form of God,

did not regard equality with God something to be grasped.
Rather, he emptied himself,
taking the form of a slave,
coming in human likeness;
and found human in appearance,
he humbled himself,
becoming obedient to death,
even death on a cross. (Phil 2:5b-8)

Though he was in the form of God, like the two in the garden, he, unlike them, was *willing* to be human. He was willing to accept all that goes with being human, the weakness and the strength. Like us in all but sin, he accepted the weakness of human nature—learning from mistakes, being wrong sometimes, being humiliated by weakness, even the final humiliation of death. He was willing to learn good and bad through living. He is the most fully human person that ever lived. He is the most complete image of God in human flesh—so full and complete that we acknowledge in faith that he is both truly God and truly human. He is God's Wisdom, come to show us how to be fully who we are, how to become all that we can be.

Consider

Do you really believe that you are an image of God?

Do you have the courage to accept that truth?

Prayer

The prayer for the feast of the Transfiguration in the Sacramentary shows us our hope:

God, our Father,
In the transfigured glory of Christ your Son,
You strengthen our faith by confirming the witness of
    your prophets
And show us the splendor of your beloved sons and
    daughters.
As we listen to the voice of your Son,
Help us to become heirs to eternal life with him.
This we ask through the Holy Spirit,
Who lives and reigns with you, one God, forever
    and ever.

Wisdom in the Daily, Part 1
Eating and Drinking; Possessions

There is an appointed time for everything,
  and a time for every affair under the heavens.
A time to give birth, and a time to die;
  a time to plant, and a time to uproot the plant.
A time to kill, and a time to heal;
  a time to tear down, and a time to build.
A time to weep, and a time to laugh;
  a time to mourn, and a time to dance.
A time to scatter stones, and a time to gather them;
  a time to embrace, and a time to be far from embraces.
A time to seek, and a time to lose;
  a time to keep, and a time to cast away.
A time to rend, and a time to sew;
  a time to be silent, and a time to speak.
A time to love, and a time to hate;
  a time of war, and a time of peace. (Eccl 3:1-8)

 isdom is the most incarnational part of the
Old Testament; it is the revelation of God
in common, daily human experience. Pearl

Bailey is said to have observed that the trouble with life is that it's so daily! For most of us, the place where we encounter God is in daily life, in all those times Qoheleth is talking about in the passage above. (Note: Qoheleth is this sage's Hebrew name and Ecclesiastes is his Greek name.) The sage concludes that "there is nothing better for us than to rejoice and to do well during life. Moreover, that all can eat and drink and enjoy the good of all their toil—this is a gift of God" (Eccl 3:13). So where do we find God? In all the times of our lives, in the stories of our daily lives. Every day we choose, a thousand times a day, to enjoy what God has given us and to find God in the circumstances of our daily lives.

Attention to the daily is certainly a monastic value as well. Benedict exhorts his followers to "open our eyes to the light that comes from God and our ears to the voice from heaven that *every day* calls out this charge: 'If you hear God's voice today, do not harden your hearts'" (Ps 95:8; RB Prol.9-10, italics mine). He also reminds us that "the Lord waits for us *daily* to translate into action . . . his holy teachings" (Prol.35, italics mine). Most of Benedict's Rule has to do with daily life.

We will consider daily life in three areas: (1) eating and drinking; (2) possessions; and (3) relationships. This chapter will deal with the first two areas. A later chapter will be devoted to relationships. So what can we say about eating and drinking? Ben Sira gives us good advice:

> Are you seated at the table of the great?
>   Bring to it no greedy gullet,
> Nor say, "How much food there is here!"
>   Remember that the greedy eye is evil.
> What has been created more greedy than the eye?
>   Therefore, it weeps for any cause.

> Eat, like anyone else, what is set before you,
>> but do not eat greedily, lest you be despised.
> Be the first to stop, as befits good manners;
>> and do not gorge yourself, lest you give offense.
> If there are many with you at table,
>> do not be the first to stretch out your hand.
>>> (Sir 31:12-13, 16-18)

The old sage sounds a bit like Miss Manners or Ann Landers. Don't grab the mashed potatoes before someone else has a chance for some. Don't eat like you are starved! But Ben Sira's advice is deeper than these table manners we learned as children. The goal of wisdom, as we know, is the good life. We sit at the table—every table—as if we were at the eternal banquet, caring for our neighbor as we will at that great feast. Ben Sira asks, "Are you seated at the table of the great?" Indeed we are! We always are. My great-aunt Samantha always used the good dishes when we visited her. She said, "Who is more important than my family?" The table is one place where we daily show reverence to one another.

Ben Sira is also concerned about moderation:

> Does not a little suffice for a well-bred person?
>> When he lies down, he does not wheeze.
> Moderate eating ensures sound slumber
>> and a clear mind on rising the next day.
> The distress of sleeplessness and of nausea
>> and colic are with the glutton!
>
> Listen to me, my child, and do not scorn me;
>> later you will find my advice good.
> In whatever you do, be moderate,
>> and no sickness will befall you. (Sir 31:19-20, 22)

The motivation offered by the sage is both practical and encouraging: "Enjoy the good life! Have a wonderful dinner!

But don't eat too much or you'll make yourself sick. One piece of pie is grand. Eating the whole pie is not only unwise; it is also most certainly not the good life."

St. Benedict offers much of the same advice. The Rule indicates that he knows the significance of eating and drinking. Terrence Kardong observes, "To judge from the sheer extent of Benedict's remarks on meals and food, the subject is quite important to him."[1] Benedict provides for sufficient food and sufficient variety—two kinds of cooked food, plus possibly a third dish—but warns that "above all, gluttony be avoided and the monk never be surprised by indigestion" (RB 39.7).[2]

Moderation is the principle regarding drink for both Ben Sira and Benedict.

> Let not wine be the proof of your strength,
>> for wine has been the ruin of many.
> As the furnace tests the work of the smith,
>> so does wine the hearts of the insolent.
> Wine is very life to anyone,
>> if taken in moderation.
> Does anyone really live who lacks the wine
>> which from the beginning was created for joy?
> Joy of heart, good cheer, and delight
>> is wine enough, drunk at the proper time. (Sir 31:25-28)

Regarding drink, Benedict too is a realist. He recommends that monastics not drink at all, "but since monks in our day cannot be convinced of this, let us at least agree not to drink to excess" (RB 40.6).[3]

---

[1] Terrence Kardong, *Benedict's Rule: A Translation and Commentary* (Collegeville, MN: Liturgical Press, 1996), 338.

[2] Kardong's translation, from ibid., 322.

[3] Ibid., 327.

Ben Sira's final advice is to be grateful to God for all these good gifts. As Qoheleth said, "That all can eat and drink and enjoy the good of all their toil—this is a gift of God" (Eccl 3:13). There is a time to eat and drink and a time to fast, but all times are times of moderation. St. Benedict adds, there is never to be any murmuring (RB 40.8-9; 41.5). All times are times of kindness, generosity, and consideration of others. This indeed is the good life.

It is also worth remembering, as we consider eating and drinking, that Jesus too enjoyed good food and drink. It has been observed that there is no recorded instance of Jesus refusing an invitation to dinner. His enemies even called him a drunkard and a glutton (Matt 11:19; Luke 7:34). Robert Karris points out that someone either eats or talks about food in every chapter of the Gospel of Luke and that often Jesus is the one eating.[4] Ponder this insight! In the Gospel of Luke how do the disciples recognize the risen Christ? The two walking with him on the way to Emmaus recognize him in the breaking of the bread (Luke 24:30-31). When Christ appears to the eleven in the upper room the disciples are terrified until Jesus says, "Do you have anything to eat?" Then they say, "Oh, it's you!" (Luke 24:36-43, loosely translated). Most important, the memorial Jesus gave us so that we might continue to enjoy his presence is a meal. "Eat and drink," he says, "and *whenever* you do this, do it in memory of me" (see Luke 22:19-20, italics mine). At every meal we share we are called to find God, to find the risen Christ. Indeed this is the good life.

A second area of daily life where moderation is necessary is the area of possessions. What do we do with the

---

[4] Robert J. Karris, *Eating Your Way through Luke's Gospel* (Collegeville, MN: Liturgical Press, 2006).

stuff we have? Ben Sira has three pieces of advice regarding our possessions: (1) be content with what you have; (2) be generous with others; and (3) be gentle with yourself. First, be content with what you have:

> Life's prime needs are water, bread, and clothing,
>   and also a house for decent privacy.
> Better is the life of the poor under the shadow of their
>   own roof
>   than sumptuous banquets among strangers.
> Whether little or much, be content with what you have:
>   then you will hear no reproach as a parasite.
>   (Sir 29:21-23)

Proverbs has similar advice and gives us a very useful prayer:

> Put falsehood and lying far from me,
>   give me neither poverty nor riches;
>   provide me only with the food I need;
> Lest, being full, I deny you,
>   saying, "Who is the Lord?"
> Or, being in want, I steal,
>   and profane the name of my God. (Prov 30:8-9)

Other wise people give us similar advice. St. Francis de Sales says, "Ask for nothing; refuse nothing." Columba Stewart, OSB, gave me a similar definition of asceticism: "Take only what you need." That is much more difficult than it sounds. It is so tempting to take more, but it is equally tempting to take less in order to appear disciplined. But moderation is genuine asceticism and genuine wisdom. This is the good life recommended by the Acts of the Apostles: "All who believed were together and had all things in common; they would sell their property and possessions and divide them among all according to each one's need" (Acts 2:44-45).

It is an excellent description of the biblical *shalom*, where everyone has what is needed for a full life. What better description do we have of heaven?

St. Benedict encourages us to call nothing our own, not even our bodies (RB 58.24-25), but he also instructs the superior to give us everything we need (RB 55.18-19). He also emphasizes the warning that we should avoid murmuring at any cost. The question of what we really need is where the difficulty arises. Once in conversation I happened to mention that I was embarrassed because I had so much! A friend (not a community member) was amazed by this comment, reflecting that in our culture the more "stuff" we have, the better off we are. But that is a false assumption. "Stuff" accumulates and then occupies more and more of our space and time to take care of it. A novice once commented that she had decided the community loved most the sister who died with the least "stuff." I still wonder which comes first, the love or the ability to be detached from possessions.

Ben Sira's second recommendation regarding possessions is to be generous to others:

> Lose your money for relative or friend;
>   do not hide it under a stone to rot.
> Dispose of your treasure according to the commandments
>   of the Most High,
>   and that will profit you more than the gold.
> Store up almsgiving in your treasury,
>   and it will save you from every evil.
> Better than a mighty shield and a sturdy spear
>   it will fight for you against the enemy. (Sir 29:10-13;
>   see also 29:1-3, 8-9)

He declares that generosity to others will save you from every evil and is indeed a guarantee of life. What can be worth more than that!

Finally, Ben Sira advises us to be gentle with ourselves. In reality this is a manifestation of humility—knowing who we are and what we need—and an expression of that genuine asceticism of taking what we need and only that. The sage warns: "None are worse than those who are stingy with themselves. . . . If ever they do good, it is by mistake; in the end they reveal their meanness" (Sir 14:6, 7). This is the alternative that he recommends:

> [I]f you have the means, treat yourself well,
>   and enjoy life as best you can.
> Remember that death does not delay,
>   and you have not been told the grave's appointed time.
> Before you die, be good to your friends;
>   give them a share in what you possess.
> Do not deprive yourself of good things now
>   or let a choice portion escape you.
> Will you not leave your riches to others,
>   and your earnings to be divided by lot?
> Give and take, treat yourself well,
>   for in Sheol there are no joys to seek. (Sir 14:11-16)

Ben Sira, we must remember, did not believe in life after death, and we do. But the sage's advice is still worth considering. Do not wait to enjoy life; enjoy the present moment. The joys of the present are God's gift to us, as Qoheleth tells us. It is in the present that we find the presence of God. Finding God in the present is both our delight and the discipline that leads to freedom, that allows us to be fully alive. It is certain that today we will hear God's voice and see God's face. Today, in this very present moment, we are called to let our hard hearts be softened with gratitude and awe for all the good gifts God gives us.

Consider

What are your challenges regarding moderation in eating and drinking?

What possessions do you have stowed away that you have not used in years?

How does the advice of the sages help you deal with these challenges?

Prayer

All-provident God,
thank you for all your good gifts.
Help me to use them wisely
and to share with others generously,
so that we may all come happily
to your eternal banquet.

Listening
The Way to Wisdom

St. Benedict begins his Rule with the exhortation to "listen with the ear of our hearts." To be wise is to be people who know how to listen. Take a quiet moment to remember a time when you received the gift of someone listening to you. Really listening! The skill of genuine listening is scarce in our society. We are bombarded by so many sounds, all clamoring for our attention. We have learned all too well how to tune out all this distraction, so we are in danger of also tuning out the voices that are essential for us to hear. Knowing how to listen and to whom is a major skill in becoming wise, a major element in learning how to live the good life. In my professional career I taught both music and language, both areas in which listening is essential. It is a struggle to teach students how to listen, how to learn and find delight through their ears. We are all very good with the mute button, canceling out the voices of each other and thus also canceling out the voice of God. But if we are going to be wise, we must learn to cherish this

41

gift of listening. Think for a moment of the wise person you remembered in chapter 1. Isn't that wise person someone who knows how to listen? Sirach says, "Happy is the one who finds a friend, who speaks to listening ears" (Sir 25:9).

If we are privileged to pray the Liturgy of the Hours together, the psalms that we pray every day teach us to listen. The psalms are, as we know, the word of God. God speaks to us through the psalms as through all of Scripture. So we who pray the psalms are becoming, slowly but surely, people who listen to the voice of God. But how do we hear God's voice? Day after day, as we pray the Liturgy of the Hours, we hear the voice of God in the voices of those who are praying with us. What does that teach us about listening to our brothers and sisters at other times? We each hear the word of God differently. If we are going to listen to the voice of God, we must each learn how to listen to each other.

Listening is one of the most significant ways to wisdom, a necessary skill to arrive at the good life. The first few verses of the book of Proverbs tell us that those who listen to this collection of wise sayings will learn about wisdom and instruction, understand words of insight, gain instruction in wise dealing, righteousness, justice, and equity. The simple will learn shrewdness; the young will learn knowledge and prudence. The wise will also hear and acquire skill to understand proverbs and riddles (see Prov 1:2-6). All this comes from listening!

It is essential for us to listen not only to each other but especially to the poorest and the least. These little ones are those to whom God listens. The psalms tell us this: "O, LORD, you have heard the desire of the poor. You strengthen their hearts; you turn your ear" (Ps 10:17). Again we are assured, "[T]ruly God has listened, and has heeded the voice of my prayer" (Ps 66:19). In Bertolt Brecht's play *The Caucasian Chalk Circle*, Grusche, the nurse for the governor's child, is caught at a moment of grave danger. A revolution has broken out and the governor has been killed. His wife has fled, abandoning the child. Grusche is about to flee also when she hears the child cry. Then the chorus says to her:

> Consider this, those who do not heed a cry for help
> But pass by with distracted ear
> Will never again hear the hushed call of a lover,
> the blackbird in the morning
> Or the contented sigh of the tired grapepickers at angelus.[1]

If we do not hear the cry of the poor, neither will we hear the voice of the God who does hear their cry. There is no such thing as selective deafness. If we close our ears to what we do not want to hear, neither will we hear what we do want.

The Wisdom Woman tells us that those who listen to her will be happy. If we listen to her, we will hear the voice of God, the voice that leads us to life (Prov 8:34-35). How can our ears be attuned to hear this life-giving message? We listen to God's voice in the voices of the poor and vulnerable. We are sometimes blessed by hearing God's word in the voices of our family and friends, even if it is a difficult word. Qoheleth reminds us that "it is better to listen to the rebuke of the wise / than to listen to the song of fools" (Eccl 7:5). We also hear God's voice in the depths of our hearts. Sirach advises us that the counsel of our own hearts is more reliable that "seven sentinels on a tower" (Sir 37:13-14).

---

[1] Bertolt Brecht, *Der Kaukasische Kreidekreis* (Berlin & Frankfurt am Main: Surkampf, 1963), 38; (original written 1944/1945) Act 1, Scene 2: "Wisse, Frau, wer einen Hilferuf nicht hört / Sondern vorbeigeht, verstörten Ohrs: nie mehr / Wird der hören den leisen Ruf des Liebsten noch / Im Morgengrauen die Amsel oder den wohligen/ Seufzer der erschöpften Weinpflucker beim Angelus." Translation mine.

Wisdom comes to us from God in prayer, from other wise people, and from our own experience. If we wish to be attuned to this wisdom, however, we must cultivate another virtue: silence. The book of Proverbs warns us against too much talking: "Where words are many, sin is not wanting; / but those who restrain their lips do well" (Prov 10:19); and elsewhere, "death and life are in the power of the tongue" (Prov 18:21a). There is a positive side also in perceptive silence:

> Those who spare their words are truly knowledgeable,
>   and those who are discreet are intelligent.
> Even fools, keeping silent, are considered wise;
>   if they keep their lips closed, intelligent. (Prov 17:27-28)

Or as the modern proverb has it: "Better to be silent and be thought a fool than to speak and prove it!"

The practice of silence is essential if we wish to be wise. If we do not know how to be truly silent, how can we hear one another? In her book *Lost in Wonder*, Esther de Waal describes the discipline of silence.[2] True silence begins with the discipline of sitting still. Then, gently, we must empty our minds of all the rattling and rustling that usually fills them. We let go of the worry about what we must accomplish today and surrender the good and bad of yesterday into God's hands. We learn to breathe slowly and deeply. If we are fortunate enough to be outside, we let the fragrances of plants and the songs of birds fill our emptiness. We delight in the presence of God. Most of us, however, can manage this surrender only briefly. But a regular practice of cultivating silence—daily, if possible—can result in surprising blessings both in our physical being and our mental state. The reward is amazing.

---

[2] Esther de Waal, *Lost in Wonder* (Collegeville, MN: Liturgical Press, 2003), 37–55.

Silence, however, is ambiguous. There is the good silence described above, but there is also a foolish and cowardly silence in the face of injustice. Qoheleth observes, there is "a time to be silent and a time to speak" (Eccl 3:7). It is true wisdom to know the difference. Genuine silence is usually the prerequisite to genuine listening.

The ability to be silent is a characteristic of the wise, but silence is not easy to learn. My novice director (the sister who was responsible for training me in living a monastic life) once told me that silence was not my predominant virtue! She was, of course, quite correct. She could well have quoted Sirach: "Let anything you hear die with you; / never fear, it will not make you burst!" (Sir 19:10). But now I know the dead feeling I have at the end of a day of constant talking, and I realize that silence is a gift we give each other. It is a fragile gift, threatened by noise outside us and within us. An even greater threat to listening and thus to gaining wisdom is the inner noise: worry, planning everything I have to do today, nursing hurt feelings or anger, or just talking to myself. Silence is a gift we give, not only to others, but also to ourselves. But silence, like all freedoms, is a discipline that must be learned and practiced. Ultimately, silence is a gift God gives us; we beg God daily for the gift of a quiet heart. Without silence we will never be able to listen to each other, to the poor, to God.

Scripture tells us that genuine listening is even part of our being like God. We were created in God's image, and now we pray to grow more and more into that likeness of God. The story of Elijah's contest with the prophets of Baal reminds us that God is indeed a great listener (1 Kgs 18:21-39). Elijah challenges the prophets of Baal to a liturgical duel. Each side should prepare a sacrifice to its respective god. Each should stack the wood for the fire, sacrifice a young bull, lay the carcass on the wood, but not light the fire. Whichever god lit the fire would be god in Israel. The prophets of Baal prepared the sacrifice, prayed, and danced around the altar all morning, but nothing happened. The narrator observes, "[T]here was no sound, no one answering, no one listening" (1 Kgs 18:29). When Elijah prepared the sacrifice in the afternoon, paradoxically even pouring water over it, the "Lord's fire came down and devoured the burnt offering, wood, stones, and dust and lapped up the water in the trench" (1 Kgs 18:38). Clearly the God who is listening is the "Lord, God of Abraham, Isaac, and Israel."

The psalms assure us over and over that our God is the God who is listening. God is not like the idols who "have ears but they cannot hear" (Ps 115:6; cf. 94:9; 135:17). God stoops down to hear our cry (Ps 40:2; cf. 34:18; 145:19). The turn to hope in most laments comes because God hears us! One of my students observed this about the singer of Psalm 116: "No wonder this guy is so happy! God heard him on the day he called (see Ps 116:1-2)! I usually have to wait weeks!" God shows us that listening is not a passive activity. When God listens, God acts. Listening is an active, attentive work that has consequences. True listening means we will be changed; we too will have to act.

So it should come as no surprise that the first word in the Rule of Benedict is "Listen." The Rule of Benedict is itself a work of wisdom literature, based on biblical wisdom and common human experience. Daniel Ward, OSB, himself a wise person, once said that everything else we are told in the Rule is to enable us to listen. We are called to simplify our lives and clear our ears and hearts so we can truly listen. But listening leads to action. Benedict follows his comment about listening with the call to obedience: "The labor of obedience will bring you back to [God] from whom you had drifted through the sloth of disobedience" (RB Prol.2). This call is true to the sense of obedience in the Hebrew Scriptures. In Hebrew there is no word for "obey." The concept is conveyed through the idiom "to hear the voice of." God calls to us every day, "Oh that today you would heed God's voice! Harden not your hearts" (Ps 95:7b-8a). The goal of this genuine listening to God's voice is the goal of wisdom: the good life. Wisdom promises us:

> Now, children, listen to me;
>   happy are they who keep my ways.
> Listen to instruction and grow wise,
>   do not reject it!
> Happy the one who listens to me,
>   attending daily at my gates,
>   keeping watch at my doorposts;
> For whoever finds me finds life,
>   and wins favor from the LORD;
> But those who pass me by do violence to themselves;
>   all who hate me love death. (Prov 8:32-36)

This goal is also the aim of the Rule of Benedict. "What . . . is more delightful than this voice of the Lord calling to us? See how the Lord in his love shows us the way of life" (RB Prol.19-20). Listening leads to life, the good life.

Consider

When have you experienced the gift of someone truly listening to you?

How did that feel?

Prayer

> God of mystery,
> it is you whom we find in the silence;
> it is you who fill our empty hearts and nourish our hunger.
> Give us listening ears
> that we may hear your voice in the voices of others,
> especially the poor and vulnerable.
> Open our hearts to your call.
> This we ask in the name of Jesus your Son.

Wisdom in the Daily, Part 2
Relationships and Reconciliation

A third significant element in our daily lives besides eating and drinking and possessions is relationships—our relationship with God and our relationship with one another. These two interactions are inextricably bound together. If we are people of wisdom, if we are going to live the good life, we are called to be people who have healthy relationships with God and with one another. This is a daily challenge in families, in community life, in our workplace. We go to God together. In chapter 72 of the Rule of Benedict we pray: "May Christ bring us *all together* to everlasting life." When I was deciding to enter monastic life, my mother asked, "Do you really think you can live with four hundred women?" I didn't bother to tell her that at that time there were actually six hundred women in the community of Mount St. Scholastica. But it does not matter how many people we live with. It can be just as difficult—perhaps more so—to live with one other person. We have all experienced this at some time or another.

Both the biblical wisdom literature and the Rule of Benedict (especially chapter 4, "Tools for Good Works") have much to say about our relationships. First of all, there are things to avoid: "Do not love *quarreling*," says Benedict in RB 4.4 (italics mine). Proverbs gives us great images to reinforce this injunction: "[T]he start of strife is like the opening of a dam; check a quarrel before it bursts forth" (Prov 17:14). Once a dam is breached, it is very difficult to restore the situation. It is all too easy in daily life to let a little disagreement—or a big hurt—turn into a lifelong bickering. Even more foolish is joining a quarrel already in progress: "Whoever meddles in the quarrel of another / is one who grabs a passing dog by the ears" (Prov 26:17).

Mother Lucy Dooley, prioress of Mount St. Scholastica in the first part of the twentieth century, reportedly heard two sisters arguing in the hall. She said to one: "Tell her you are sorry." Then she said to the other: "Tell her you were wrong." Spend some time with that conversation. Does anyone win or lose?

Often quarreling comes from what we *say*. Benedict advises: "Guard your lips from harmful or deceptive speech" (RB 4.51). It is so hard to keep still, especially when we have a juicy story or a justifiable murmur. Proverbs says, "The words of a talebearer are like dainty morsels: / they sink into one's inmost being" (Prov 26:22). Sometimes it is true that we delight in a "justifiable" murmur, but "[w]hoever gloats over evil will be destroyed, / and whoever repeats gossip has no sense" (Sir 19:5-6). St. Benedict clearly does not like murmuring, repeating the prohibition about thirteen times. But paradoxically, there is also good "gossip" and good "murmuring." Psalm 1 says we will be happy if we murmur God's law day and night. The Hebrew word here is usually translated "meditate," but its basic meaning is "murmur" or "mutter." Also, the etymology of the English word "gossip" is *sip* (sibling) of God, or Godmother, who should be repeating *good* stories! That paradox is also worth pondering for some time.

Wicked gossip and nasty murmuring can lead us to *rash judgment*. Sirach advises:

> Before investigating, do not find fault;
>   examine first, then criticize.
> Before listening, do not say a word,
>   interrupt no one in the midst of speaking.
> Do not dispute about what is not your concern;
>   in the quarrels of the arrogant do not take part.
>   (Sir 11:7-9)

It is all too easy to pick up half the truth or to criticize with no reason, all too easy to get into disputes over decisions that are not ours to make. Why does she always insist that we take the longer road? Why does he leave the newspaper in such a mess? Why was our coworker fired? Why do we always sing the same hymn in church? Why not? None of us is responsible for every decision. We expect the responsibility to be fairly divided. Why do we not let it be?

Quarreling, gossip, murmuring, rash judgment all divide us. They are a failure in wisdom, which, like a bridge, unites us. They are a failure in righteousness, which is honoring the demands of every relationship. They destroy the good life. No other thing can substitute for healthy, life-giving relationships—not even eat, drink, and be merry! "Better a dish of herbs where love is than a fatted ox and hatred with it" (Prov 15:17).

Disputes and misunderstandings arise in every healthy relationship, however. So we have a need for reconciliation and healing. We are called to be like God, "gracious and merciful, slow to anger and rich in love" (cf. Jonah 4:2). Compare Psalms 111 and 112. Psalm 111 describes God as "gracious and merciful," and Psalm 112 turns around to declare that the righteous person is "generous" and "loving" (Ps 111:4; 112:4). In my community we have developed a ceremony to ritualize this reconciliation. First we remember stories of the past. Then we go one by one to a person in authority who asks us, "Do you forgive the community for any way it has hurt you? In the name of the community I forgive you for any way you may have hurt the community." There are surely ways to do this in a family also, both formally and informally. However we accomplish this task, it is essential that we reconcile our differences and forgive our hurts.

What does the wisdom literature teach us about reconciliation? First, speech must be gentle. Proverbs advises us that "a mild answer turns back wrath" (Prov 15:1) but also asserts paradoxically that "a soft tongue can break a bone" (Prov 25:15). That is a puzzling adage to ponder. St. Benedict tells his followers that we should "prefer moderation in speech" (RB 4.52) and describes the eleventh step of humility as speaking gently, briefly, reasonably, without raising the voice (RB 7.60).

If confrontation is necessary, however —and it is better than brooding over wrongs—it should be done directly, with compassion and a willingness to be wrong about the offense. Benedict tells us that no one has the authority to excommunicate or strike another unless it has been given by the superior (RB 70.2). This is what Sirach advises when, as Alexander Di Lella says, you "hear unsavory stories about friends."[1]

> Admonish your friend—he may not have done it;
> and if he did, that he may not do it again.

---

[1] Alexander Di Lella and Patrick Skehan, *The Wisdom of Ben Sira*, AB 39 (New York: Doubleday, 1987), 293.

Admonish your neighbor—he may not have said it;
  and if he did, that he may not say it again.
Admonish your friend—often it may be slander;
  do not believe every story.
Then, too, a person can slip and not mean it;
  who has not sinned with his tongue?
Admonish your neighbor before you break with him;
  and give due place to the Law of the Most High.
    (Sir 19:13-17)

Sirach is relying on Leviticus: "You shall not hate any of your kindred in your heart. Reprove your neighbor openly so that you do not incur sin because of that person. Take no revenge and cherish no grudge against your own people. You shall love your neighbor as yourself. I am the LORD" (Lev 19:17-18).

As a wise teacher, Sirach will appeal to God's law even more strongly in his call for forgiveness:

Forgive your neighbor the wrong done to you;
  then when you pray, your own sins will be forgiven.
Does anyone nourish anger against another
  and expect healing from the Lord?
Can one refuse mercy to a sinner like oneself,
  yet seek pardon for one's own sins?
If a mere mortal cherishes wrath,
  who will forgive his sins?
Remember your last days and set enmity aside;
  remember death and decay, and cease from sin!
Remember the commandments and do not be angry with
    your neighbor;
  remember the covenant of the Most High, and overlook
    faults. (Sir 28:2-7)

This instruction anticipates the Lord's Prayer: "Forgive us our trespasses as we forgive those who trespass against us" (see Matt 6:12; Luke 11:4). The insight that when we forgive one another God forgives us is an integral part of Jewish teaching (see the *Testimony of the Twelve Patriarchs:* Gad vi 3-7 and Zebulon v 3; *Rosh Ha-shanah*, 17a).[2]

If we are looking for the good life, we will speak gently, confront honestly, and be eager to forgive. Even this, however, is not enough. We are called to be the bridge, to reach out actively to bring peace, *shalom*, that situation where everyone has what is necessary for a full life. We are called to reach out particularly to those most in need.

First of all, the needs of elderly parents and other elders such as those in community put great demands on us. Care of those who have nourished our lives, when we were children or perhaps newcomers to the monastery, is definitely part of the good life. Benedict reminds us that our elders should be treated with kind consideration (RB 37.3). This instruction is already present in Sirach:

> [B]e steadfast in honoring your father;
> 　do not grieve him as long as he lives.
> Even if his mind fails, be considerate of him;
> 　do not revile him because you are in your prime.
> Kindness to a father will not be forgotten;
> 　it will serve as a sin offering—it will take lasting root.
> In time of trouble it will be recalled to your advantage,
> 　like warmth upon frost it will melt away your sins.
> Those who neglect their father are like blasphemers;
> 　those who provoke their mother are accursed by their
> 　　Creator. (Sir 3:12-16)

The poor are another special category who deserve our generosity. Again, there are poor within our families or within the monastery as well as without; we need to find

---

[2] References from ibid., 363–64.

them. Proverbs reminds us that we sin if we despise the hungry, but we will be happy if we are kind to the poor (Prov 14:21). But again it is Sirach who is especially attentive to the poor:

> My child, do not mock the life of the poor;
>   do not keep needy eyes waiting.
> Do not grieve the hungry,
>   nor anger the needy.
> Do not aggravate a heart already angry,
>   nor delay giving to the needy.
> A beggar's request do not reject;
>   do not turn your face away from the poor.
> From the needy do not turn your eyes;
>   do not give them reason to curse you.
> If in their pain they cry out bitterly,
>   their Rock will hear the sound of their cry. (Sir 4:1-6)

Or as Benedict reminds us, "Never . . . turn away when someone needs your love" (RB 4.25-26). This injunction is not always easy! Sirach warns us not to ruin a gift by harsh words like "Get a job!" (see Sir 18:15). On the contrary he advises that "the kind word means more than the gift" (Sir 18:15-17), as Benedict reminds the cellarer (RB 31.14). Leon Bloy once said, "Be kind, be kind and you will be saints."

Even this kindness to those in need is still not enough, however, for the fullness of the good life. The crown of our relationships is friendship. Friendship is one of God's greatest gifts to us and true friendships are at least part of the glue that holds a community together.

Again we turn to Sirach, who tells us that "pleasant speech multiplies friends" (Sir 6:5). His praise of friendship warms the heart:

> Faithful friends are a sturdy shelter;
>   whoever finds one finds a treasure.

> Faithful friends are beyond price,
>> no amount can balance their worth.
> Faithful friends are life-saving medicine;
>> those who fear God will find them.
> Those who fear the Lord enjoy stable friendship,
>> for as they are, so will their neighbors be. (Sir 6:14-17)

As you are, so are your friends. Our friends help us to be faithful to God and faithful to community. Lifelong friends are truly a treasure. As Sirach says in another place:

> Do not abandon old friends;
>> new ones cannot equal them.
> A new friend is like new wine—
>> when it has aged, you drink it with pleasure. (Sir 9:10)

The advice he gives us shows us how to live together and how to enjoy the rich gift of relationships:

> As best you can, answer your neighbor,
>> and associate with the wise.
> With the learned exchange ideas;
>> and let all your conversation be about the law of the
>>> Most High.
> Take the righteous for your table companions;
>> and let your glory be in the fear of God. (Sir 9:14-16)

Finally, this wise sage Ben Sira summarizes his wisdom with a recipe or rule of thumb for the good life with regard to relationships. Following his habitual pattern, he offers us threefold advice:

> [A]ssociate with a religious person,
>> who you know keeps the commandments;
> Who is like-minded with yourself
>> and will grieve for you if you fall.

Then, too, heed your own heart's counsel;
    for there is nothing you can depend on more.
The heart can reveal your situation
    better than seven sentinels on a tower.
Then with all this, pray to God
    to make your steps firm in the true path. (Sir 37:12-15)

Three relationships: Associate with a holy person who is both faithful and compassionate, not one who is "holier than thou," but someone who understands our weakness and helps us to be strong. Listen to your own heart, your own conscience. Who is more faithful to you than it is? Third, pray to God who teaches us the way to truth. This advice is truly a description of the good life. We see it in healthy families and in the blessings of friendship. Monastics will recognize it as a description of a holy community.

A final word on the healthy relationships that are necessary for the good life comes from St. Benedict:

> Just as there is a wicked zeal of bitterness which separates from God and leads to hell, so there is a good zeal which separates from evil and leads to God and everlasting life. This, then, is the good zeal which monastics must foster with fervent love: They should each try to be the first to show respect to the other (Rom 12:10), supporting with the greatest patience one another's weaknesses of body or behavior, and earnestly competing in obedience to one another. No one is to pursue what he [or she] judges better for himself [or herself], but instead, what [is] better for someone else. To their fellow monastics they show the pure love of brothers [and sisters]; to God, loving fear; to their superior, unfeigned and humble love. Let them prefer nothing whatever to Christ, and may he bring us all together to everlasting life. (RB 72)

In his commentary on the Lord's Prayer, Cyprian says that we prefer nothing whatever to Christ because he has preferred nothing to us.[3] We learn to love one another because he has loved us so very much. So we pray, "May Christ bring us *all together* to everlasting life." Even in death we do not go alone; we go "all together." We have been on a lifelong journey together and now we see the goal: eternal life with Christ. The journey demands patience of us as we share together in the sufferings of Christ. He suffered for us that we might share in his glory. Following him on this journey takes us on a long road. Our Sister Edmunda knew this as she was dying at the age of ninety-seven. It took her some time to die, so one night one of the sisters was encouraging her: "Just let Jesus take you to heaven." Sister Edmunda replied, "It's a long trip!" And so it is. The goal, however, is worth much more than the cost. May Christ, who goes before us, "bring us *all together* to everlasting life!" (RB 72.12, italics mine).

Consider

What are the relationships that nourish your life?

Take time today to thank those who love you.

Or are there conflicts in your life—old or new—that have been left unresolved?

Do you have the courage and the humility to mend the rift?

[3] Cyprian, *De dominica oratione* (The Lord's Prayer) 15, in *Saint Cyprian: Treatises*, Fathers of the Church 36 (New York: Fathers of the Church, Inc., 1958), 140.

Prayer

Gracious and merciful God,
teach us to honor all those with whom we come in contact.
Open our hearts to mend conflict and to be grateful to
those who love us.
Bring us all together into your healing embrace.
This we ask in the name of Jesus, who prayed that we
might all be one.

Wisdom and Joy

When I was a novice my director said to me, "Joy, you know, is a gift of the Holy Spirit and sadness is not." She was responding to my attempt to go around looking holy, which I thought meant to look somber. Obviously it wasn't working! Her wise advice to me has served me throughout my life.

Take a moment to remember the wise person you pondered at the beginning of this book. Is this a person who knows true joy? What does that joy look like? What is it that brings your wise person joy? How would you define joy? What keeps that faithful river of joy flowing through your wise person even when life is hard? The biblical wisdom literature has quite a bit to say about joy. Joy, genuine gladness, is a characteristic of wise persons.

Joy is a gift of the Holy Spirit, as my novice director reminded me. It is a gift of Wisdom. Proverbs says, "Happy the one who finds wisdom, / the one who gains understanding" (Prov 3:13). The author of the book of Wisdom presents Solomon declaring,

> I determined to take [Wisdom] to live with me,
> knowing that she would be my counselor while all
>   was well,
> and my comfort in care and grief. . . .
> For association with her involves no bitterness
> and living with her no grief,
> but rather joy and gladness. (Wis 8:9, 16)

Ben Sira cannot say enough about the joy of living with Wisdom. He calls her by her other name, "Fear of the Lord."

> The fear of the Lord is glory and exultation,
> gladness and a festive crown.
> The fear of the Lord rejoices the heart,
> giving gladness, joy, and long life.
> Those who fear the Lord will be happy at the end,
> even on the day of death they will be blessed. (Sir 1:11-13)

Joy is a gift given to us by Wisdom, but joy is also a choice. We can refuse it, or we can take the risk to accept it. Qoheleth—even "vanity-of-vanities" Qoheleth—is one of the great preachers of choosing joy. In reality he is exhorting us to choose life! Seven times he encourages us. Here are some examples:

> There is nothing better for mortals than to eat and drink and provide themselves with good things from their toil. Even this, I saw, is from the hand of God. For who can eat or drink apart from God? (2:24-25)

> Therefore I praised joy, because there is nothing better for mortals under the sun than to eat and to drink and to be joyful; this will accompany them in their toil through the limited days of life God gives them under the sun. (8:15)

> Go, eat your bread with joy and drink your wine with a merry heart, because it is now that God favors your

works. At all times let your garments be white, and
spare not the perfume for your head. Enjoy life with
the wife you love, all the days of the vain life granted
you under the sun. This is your lot in life, for the toil
of your labors under the sun. (9:7-9)

Pema Chodron, an American Buddhist nun, was moved
by a retreat in which the director "emphasized joy." She
observes, "I hadn't realized how much emphasis I had put
on suffering in my own practice. I had focused on coming
to terms with the unpleasant, unacceptable, embarrassing,
and painful things that I do. In the process, I had very subtly forgotten about joy."[1] She observes that joy is a choice,
a way to learn to live well; choosing joy even gives us "a
new way of looking at suffering." Chodron tells the story
of a woman fleeing from tigers. She finally climbs partway
down a cliff and clings to some vines. Then she sees tigers
below her too. Even worse, there is a mouse chewing on the
vines she is clutching. All seems lost. But then the woman
sees a few strawberries within her reach. She takes one and
delights in its sweetness. Chodron observes:

> Tigers above, tigers below. This is actually the predica-
> ment that we are always in, in terms of our birth and
> death. Each moment is just what it is. It might be the
> only moment of our life; it might be the only straw-
> berry we'll ever eat. We could get depressed about
> it, or we could finally appreciate it and delight in the
> preciousness of every single moment of our life.[2]

[1] Pema Chodron, "Joy," from *The Wisdom of No Escape*, as excerpted
in *Wise Women*, ed. Susan Cahill (New York: W. W. Norton & Company,
1996), 377.
[2] Ibid., 378.

Chodron's story of the strawberries is an encouragement to enjoy the gift of the present moment. When Qoheleth talks about the "appointed time for everything" (3:1), his point is not so much that we must figure out what is the "right time." He actually says that we cannot know what that right time is. What he advises us to do is to receive the present moment as a gift of God, whether what it brings is delightful or tragic. The choice to find joy in the present moment takes courage, but it is all we have. We cannot change the past, nor can we usually control the future. Qoheleth says that anyone to whom God gives good things and the power to enjoy them in the present has a gift from God. Such people "will hardly dwell on the shortness of life, because God lets them busy themselves with the joy of their heart" (Eccl 5:19).

Ben Sira has strong words for those who refuse to enjoy God's gifts in the present moment or to share them with others:

> None are worse than those who are stingy with themselves;
> they punish their own avarice.
> If ever they do good, it is by mistake;
> in the end they reveal their meanness. (Sir 14:6-7)

His advice is instead to enjoy whatever we have and to be good to one another (see Sir 14:11-16). He observes that "cheerfulness prolongs [our] days" (Sir 30:22). So we see that by cultivating joy and delight, we are accepting our reality as images of God. God delights in creation, saying over and over, "How good!" (see Gen 1:4, 10, 12, 16, 21, 25, 31). God delights in everything as a parent does in a child. God is consistently imaged as a parent. God is the father begetting the mountains, the mother giving birth to the earth in Psalm 90:2. God is the father who begets the rain and dew, the mother who gives birth to the ice and hoarfrost

(Job 38:28-39). God is the father Rock that begot Israel, the mother God who gave the people birth (Deut 32:18).

All these images reveal God's delight. We pray in Psalm 104: "Let God's glory endure and the Lord delight in creating" (Ps 104:31; ICEL). Psalm 104 and Proverbs both tell us that God creates through Wisdom: "How varied are your works, Lord, / In wisdom you have made them all" (Ps 104:24). Wisdom tells us that she herself is God's delight, playing on the face of the earth and before God. She is God's delight and she delights in us (Prov 8:30-31). God even plays with chaos, the Leviathan (see Job 40:29; Ps 104:26). What a delight for us, to know that God delights in creation. Play and delight are intimately linked with Wisdom, God's Wisdom.

What does this joy look like in our ordinary lives? Where do we find it? Everything we have considered about wisdom so far tells us the answer. First of all, God has shared with us the power to create and the responsibility for creation (Gen 1:28). These gifts must go together: power and responsibility, justice and compassion. Second, the testimony of creation is a witness to our freedom, our freedom to be and our freedom to participate in creation. Isn't this freedom a cause for joy? Our God who created us and all other things tells us we have no reason to fear even primeval chaos. Chaos no longer has the power to dominate and destroy us. God has made chaos—Leviathan—into something to play with (Job 40:25-29). Walter Brueggemann says that "Israel refused the claims of chaos, refused to cringe in helplessness before the powers that negated life."[3] God has tamed chaos, corralled it so that we might have a place to live and work. This is a wonderful freedom.

---

[3] Walter Brueggemann, *Theology of the Old Testament* (Minneapolis: Fortress, 1997), 164.

Freedom in creating leads to delight for us as well as for God. We have so much that delights us: all the beauty and magnificence that God has created, the wonder of other human beings too deep for us ever to understand, our own strength and vulnerability with their gifts and flaws. We have the gift to delight in our own power to create and in what we create. Wonder and delight lead us to awe. This awe is genuine fear of the Lord, true humility.

Abraham Joshua Heschel says:

> Inquire of your soul, what does it know, what does it take for granted. It will tell you only that no-thing is taken for granted; each thing is a surprise, *being is unbelievable*. We are amazed at seeing anything at all; amazed not only at particular values and things but *at the unexpectedness of being as such*, at the fact there is being at all.[4]

In his commentary on Heschel, John Merkle adds,

> When in fact we refuse to take the world for granted, to merely accept it as given, and when, instead, we attempt to face the world as if "for the first time," then we begin to understand what Heschel means when he says: "The world is not just here. It shocks us into amazement."[5]

All of God's creation shocks us into amazement and praise and fills us with joy: "I will sing to my God, / make music for the Lord / as long as I live. / Let my song give joy to God / who is a joy to me" (Ps 104:33-34; ICEL).

[4] Abraham Joshua Heschel, *Man Is Not Alone: A Philosophy of Religion* (New York: Farrar, Straus, & Giroux, 1951), 12.

[5] John C. Merkle, *The Genesis of Faith: The Depth Theology of Abraham Joshua Heschel* (New York: Macmillan, 1985), 155–56.

So how can we claim this joy? How can we nourish and express this reverence and awe? Pema Chodron advises, "Acknowledging the preciousness of each day is a good way to live, a good way to reconnect with our basic joy."[6] St. Philip Neri reminds us of the fruits of joy: "Cheerfulness strengthens the heart and makes us persevere in a good life. Therefore the servant of God ought always to be in good spirits."[7] St. Benedict says that "as we progress in this way of life and in faith, we shall run on the path of God's commandments, our hearts overflowing with the inexpressible delight of love" (Prol.49). These are strong words. How can we learn to cultivate this joy and delight?

- First, we can follow Sirach's advice and cultivate joy in our daily lives by appreciating God's gifts and sharing them with others.

- Second, following Qoheleth's advice, we can strive to stay in the present moment, neither bemoaning the past or worrying about the future.

- Third, we can be grateful, always grateful, for everything God gives us.

- Fourth and finally, we can keep the Sabbath, taking time to delight in God's presence in creation and each other by learning to simply be. That is the purpose of Sabbath and is a Sabbath whenever we practice it. Abraham Joshua Heschel says that "even just being is being obedient because God's first command was, 'Let there be.'"[8]

[6] Chodron, "Joy," 379.
[7] www.catholictradition.org/Saints/teachings5.htm.
[8] See Abraham Joshua Heschel, *Who Is Man?* (Stanford, CA: Stanford University Press, 1965), 97–98.

This Sabbath gift is a sharing of the first created thing: time. We share it with God; we share it with creation; we share it with each other. Taking time to just "be" is a way to cultivate wonder and fear of the Lord, a way to praise God for the wonders of creation. This practice is certainly part of the good life, certainly a way to joy. Qoheleth gives us the final word: "I recognized that there is nothing better than to rejoice and to do well during life. Moreover, that all can eat and drink and enjoy the good of all their toil—this is a gift of God" (Eccl 3:12-13).

Consider

How do you cultivate a joyful spirit?

How do you give joy to others?

Prayer

Generous God, we rejoice in the gifts of love we have received from the heart of Jesus your Son. Open our hearts to share his life and continue to bless us with his love. This we ask through Jesus Christ your Son, who lives and reigns with you in the unity of the Holy Spirit, one God forever and ever.

Christ: Wisdom of God; Center of Our Lives

We have considered what wisdom is and how wise people live. Now as we come to the end of this study, I ask the crucial question: *Who* is Wisdom? It is important to know what wisdom is, but it is essential for us to recognize who Wisdom is. We meet Wisdom first in the book of Proverbs as a feminine figure, a woman. Now this may have happened simply because the Hebrew word for "wisdom," *hokmah*, is in the feminine gender. Nonetheless, the Wisdom Woman, this feminine person, becomes the strongest image of God in the Old Testament. What started out as a literary figure grows and eventually carries more truth than the original author ever guessed. The Wisdom Woman is as close to an "incarnation" of God as the Old Testament will get. How can I claim this? We must go back to the texts that describe the Wisdom Woman.

In Proverbs 1, Wisdom appears as a street prophet. She stands on the corner and calls out to passersby: "How long, you naïve ones, will you love naivete; / how long will you turn away at my reproof?" She is calling us to the good life and claims to know how to get there. Then she gives a promise: "I will pour out to you my spirit; I will acquaint you with my words" (Prov 1:22-23). Who is this person? Who is it who pours out her spirit on us and makes her words known?

Wisdom tells us more about herself in Proverbs 8. She is out on the street again, calling to anyone who is looking for the good life. Here we get a clue for where to find Wisdom—in the midst of human activity, human experience. She announces that she is the one who gives us all our skills. She says literally, "by me kings king and princes prince" (see Prov 8:15-16; the Hebrew words are from the same root). She is more precious than anything else we can imagine. "With me," she says, "are riches and honor, wealth that endures, and righteousness" (Prov 8:18). Nothing is to be preferred to her. With her you get everything else besides. This description of Wisdom anticipates Jesus' words: "Seek first the kingdom [of God] and his righteousness, and all these things will be given you besides" (Matt 6:33).

But who is this Wisdom Woman? She tells us of her origin and her task:

> The LORD begot me, the beginning of his works,
> the forerunner of his deeds of long ago;
> From of old I was formed,
> at the first, before the earth.
> When there were no deeps I was brought forth,
> when there were no fountains or springs of water;
> Before the mountains were settled into place,
> before the hills, I was brought forth;
> When the earth and the fields were not yet made,
> nor the first clods of the world.
> When he established the heavens, there was I,
> when he marked out the vault over the face of the deep;

> When he made firm the skies above,
>> when he fixed fast the springs of the deep;
> When he set for the sea its limit,
>> so that the waters should not transgress his command;
> When he fixed the foundations of earth,
>> then was I beside him as artisan. (Prov 8:22-30a)

We learn that not only was she there at the beginning of God's creation but she was God's artisan, God's designer. No wonder she claims to know how to teach us the good life! But she has more to tell us:

> I was his delight day by day,
>> playing before him all the while,
> Playing over the whole of his earth,
>> having my delight with human beings. (Prov 8:30b-32)

There is a wonderful wordplay happening here with delight and play. Wisdom is the bridge between God and the rest of us. She is God's delight and she delights in us; she plays before God and plays in the world. How do we come to God? It must be through Wisdom. Where do we find her? Where we find delight and play. This delight is fear of the Lord! This play is the good life! Wisdom tells us that this indeed is the benefit of listening to her.

> Now, children, listen to me;
>> happy are they who keep my ways.
> Listen to instruction and grow wise,
>> do not reject it!
> Happy the one who listens to me,
>> attending daily at my gates,
>> keeping watch at my doorposts;
> For whoever finds me finds life,
>> and wins favor from the Lord;
> But those who pass me by do violence to themselves;
>> all who hate me love death. (Prov 8:32-36)

To find Wisdom is to find life, to find God. To miss wisdom (the Hebrew means "to have a bad aim") is to hurt ourselves; to hate wisdom is to love death. Wisdom is the way to the good life.

So where do we find her? She fixes us dinner!

> Wisdom has built her house,
>> she has set up her seven columns;
> She has prepared her meat, mixed her wine,
>> yes, she has spread her table.
> She has sent out her maidservants; she calls
>> from the heights out over the city:
> "Let whoever is naive turn in here;
>> to any who lack sense I say,
> Come, eat of my food,
>> and drink of the wine I have mixed!
> Forsake foolishness that you may live;
>> advance in the way of understanding." (Prov 9:1-6)

Wisdom is present in every meal we eat; we find her in that most ordinary of human experiences. Proverbs tells us that she is the tree of life (Prov 3:18). She is the tree in the middle of the garden. She is both the tree of life and the tree of the knowledge of good and bad. To eat from this tree is to be wise and mature, able to distinguish between good and bad. To eat from this tree is to live.

As you ponder this glorious description of the Wisdom Woman in Proverbs, take a moment to consider the cover of this book, which is taken from one of the illuminations in *The Saint John's Bible*. Wisdom's beautifully decorated seven pillars are there. On top of each is the pearl of wisdom, an image from Job, who says: "Gold or crystal cannot equal her, . . . the value of wisdom surpasses pearls" (Job 28:17a, 18b). Toward the rear of the scene is an ornate carpet, signifying the creativity of the Wisdom Woman who "weaves with skillful hands" (Prov 31:13). The pillar closest to the front seems to grow into the tree of life, the wisdom tree who says of herself, "My fruit is better than gold, even fine gold, and my yield than choice silver" (Prov 8:19). The vertical gold and silver batons suggest that wisdom is the bond that links us with God. She is the bridge between God and humanity. She plays before God; she plays on the surface of the earth (Prov 8:30-31).

Ben Sira adds his voice to the biblical chorus of praise for Wisdom. He tells us that she comes "from the mouth of the Most High" (Sir 24:3). What comes from one's mouth? Breath; words. Wisdom is God's word, God's breath. She is everywhere, but she takes root in Zion in the midst of God's holy people (see Sir 24:3-12). She is not only the tree of life, as Proverbs tells us; she is every wonderful tree offering everything that delights the senses—beauty, fragrance, sweetness. (Eve was right when she said that the tree in the middle of the garden was good for food, pleasing to the eyes, and desirable for gaining wisdom!) Again Wisdom offers us the banquet:

> Come to me, all who desire me,
>   and be filled with my fruits.
> You will remember me as sweeter than honey,
>   better to have than the honeycomb.
> Those who eat of me will hunger still,
>   those who drink of me will thirst for more.
> Whoever obeys me will not be put to shame,
>   and those who serve me will never go astray.
>   (Sir 24:19-22)

Doesn't this sound familiar? Who is this Wisdom Woman who makes such extravagant offers? Who else makes a similar promise?

The first-century sage who wrote the book of Wisdom gives us even more clues. He claims, "all good things together

7:22 ?

came to me with her" (Wis 7:11). He praises her with twenty-one adjectives (7 x 3, perfect number times perfect number), and then he continues:

> Wisdom is mobile beyond all motion,
>   and she penetrates and pervades all things by reason
>   of her purity.
> For she is a breath of the might of God
>   and a pure emanation of the glory of the Almighty;
>   therefore nothing defiled can enter into her.
> For she is the reflection of eternal light,
>   the spotless mirror of the power of God,
>   the image of his goodness. (Wis 7:24-26)

Who is this Woman? A breath of the power of God, a pure outpouring of God's glory, the refulgence of eternal light. God is the light; she is the shining. She is a spotless mirror of the working of God. The Old Testament warns us that we cannot see the face of God and live (see Gen 32:31; Judg 6:22), but now we hear that Wisdom is the spotless mirror of God. If we cannot look at God directly, we can look at the face of Wisdom and see the face of God. She is the image of God's goodness. The sage goes on to say that she can do all things and renews all things; she is the one who makes holy souls into friends of God and prophets (Wis 7:27). Who is this?

The liturgy gives us a clue. In the Roman Lectionary on Trinity Sunday of Year C the first reading is Proverbs 8:22-31, cited above. What does it mean that the Church has chosen this reading from the wisdom literature specifically for Trinity Sunday? Who is it that claims to be the "beginning" (or "firstborn") of God's ways? Who is this who was begotten by God before anything was created—before the fountains or springs of water, before the mountains and hills, before even the first clods of dirt on the earth? All through God's creating, from the skies above to the depths of the sea, she says, "I was there!" Who is this? Who is it that claims to be the designer or artisan of God's creation?

If we ponder these questions about the Wisdom Woman, it will come as no surprise that when the New Testament writers try to explain who Christ is, they turn to this passage and other descriptions of Wisdom. The first chapter of the Gospel of John begins with the Word who was with God in the beginning: "[T]he Word was God. . . . All things came to be through him, and without him nothing came to be. What came to be through him was life, and this life was the light of the human race" (John 1:1c, 3-4). Is this not Wisdom? The real news in John's prologue, however, is that "the Word became flesh and made his dwelling among us" (John 1:14), literally "pitched his tent among us." Wisdom has become flesh. The shining of God's light, the outpouring of God's glory, the spotless mirror of God's face, the image of God's goodness has become flesh and pitched a tent among us. God comes to share our common human experience in order to share with us divine experience. As St. Irenaeus said, "He became what we are in order that we might become what he is."[1] Christ, as Paul tells us directly in 1 Corinthians, is "the power of God and the wisdom of God" (1 Cor 1:24).

Christ is at the beginning and end of our lives. Christ is also in the middle of our lives. When Thomas complains that he doesn't know how to go where Christ is going— or, in other words, that he doesn't know how to follow Christ—Christ replies, "I am the way and the truth and

[1] Irenaeus, *Against Heresies,* Preface Book 5; see Mary Ann Donovan, *One Right Reading? A Guide to Irenaeus* (Collegeville, MN: Liturgical Press, 1997), 142; Aelred Squire, *Asking the Fathers: The Art of Inspiration and Prayer* (Ramsey, NJ: Paulist Press, 1973), 23.

the life" (John 14:6). Christ, who tells us to "run while we have the light of life" (RB Prol.13; see John 12:35), is the very way on which we run. Catherine of Siena supposedly said, "All the way to heaven is heaven because he has said, 'I am the way.'"

What insights have we gained as we draw to the end of our meditation on biblical wisdom? We have recognized that true wisdom is knowing how to live well. We have pondered the amazing figure of the Wisdom Woman and rejoiced in the good news that Christ is Wisdom Incarnate. Finally, I would like to probe the insights of a singularly wise man, St. Benedict, who left us a Rule to help us learn how to live well.

The Rule of Benedict is totally Christ centered. In the Rule it is Christ who is the Lord, the King, the Shepherd, the Householder, and sometimes even the Father! It is Christ who calls us with the words of Psalm 34: "Come, children, listen to me; I will teach you the fear of the Lord" (RB Prol.12). It is Christ who will help us answer the call throughout our lives. At the very end of the Rule Benedict asks, "Are you hastening toward your heavenly home? Then with Christ's help, keep this little rule that we have written for beginners" (RB 73.8). Christ is at the beginning and end of the Rule.

Demetrius Dumm says that the "reality which is the very heart of Benedict's spirituality [is] the presence of Christ as the one in whom monastics receive the liberating love of God and through whom they are able to share that love with others."[2] Michael Casey spins it out a little more: "The heart of all monastic observance is communion with Christ realized in prayer, in love for the brothers and sisters, and in the

---

[2] Demetrius Dumm, *Cherish Christ above All* (Mahwah, NJ: Paulist Press, 1996), 44.

sacramental overlap of these relationships in the liturgy."[3] Both agree that Christ is the very center, the heart of our lives. Christ is the one who calls us, the way on which we journey, and the one we hope to meet in the radical future.

Christ is first of all present with us to guide us on the way. Christ is present in the superior, who is believed to hold the place of Christ in the monastery. Christ is present with us in the sick: "Care of the sick must rank above and before all else, so that they may truly be served as Christ, for he said: *I was sick and you visited me* (Matt 25:36), and, *What you did for one of these least ones you did for me* (Matt 25:40)" (RB 36.1-2). Have we not all had that experience that, even in tending the most cantankerous people, we suddenly get a glimpse of Christ in their suffering and their endurance? Terrence Kardong points out that we meet Christ twice in this ministry to the sick. Christ is present in the sick one, but Christ, who called himself a servant (Matt 20:28; Mark 10:45; Luke 22:27), is also present in the one who "serves" the sick (RB 36.7; see also Phil 2:7; Matt 12:18).[4]

Christ is also present in the guests who come. Benedict is so convinced of this that he tells us three times in chapter 53: "All guests who present themselves are to be welcomed as Christ, for he himself will say: *I was a stranger and you welcomed me* (Matt 25:35)" (RB 53.1). "By a bow of the head or by a complete prostration of the body, Christ is to be adored because he is indeed welcomed in the guest" (RB 53.7). "Great care and concern are to be shown in receiving poor people and pilgrims, because in them more particularly Christ is received" (RB 53.15). Finding the face of Christ in all these people is not an easy task. But if Christ is at the

---

[3] Michael Casey, *Strangers to the City* (Brewster, MA: Paraclete, 2005), 142.

[4] Terrence Kardong, *Benedict's Rule: A Translation and Commentary* (Collegeville, MN: Liturgical Press, 1996), 304.

heart of our life, we will be much happier if we help each other find Christ in these people whom he sends to us and in whom he chooses most especially to be present.

Christ teaches us the way through his words and shows us the way through his own life. Benedict exhorts us, saying that "the Lord waits for us daily to translate into action his holy teaching" (RB Prol.35). He also gives us Christ's life as an example: "The faithful must endure everything, even contradiction for the Lord's sake, saying in the person of those who suffer, *For your sake we are put to death continually; we are regarded as sheep for the slaughter*" (RB 7.38; Rom 8:36). It is for Christ's sake and following Christ's teaching that we suffer even injustice with a quiet heart.

Benedict describes what happens to us if we imitate Christ's obedience:

> It is love that impels them to pursue everlasting life; therefore they are eager to take the narrow road of which the Lord says: *Narrow is the road that leads to life* (Matt 7:14). They no longer live by their own judgment, giving in to their whims and appetites; rather they walk according to another's decisions and directions, choosing to live in monasteries and to have an abbot over them. People of this resolve unquestionably conform to the saying of the Lord: *I have come not to do my own will, but the will of him who sent me* (John 6:38). (RB 5.10-13)

We are all called to renounce ourselves in order to follow Christ, whether we are monastics or not. Jesus has said to each of us, "If anyone wishes to come after me, you must deny yourself and take up your cross daily and follow me" (RB 4.10; Matt 16:24; Luke 9:23). The road leads through the cross. There is no way we can avoid it and no way we could bear it on our own! It is only by keeping our eyes fixed on

Christ and our hearts burning with love for him that we even dare to attempt it. The way is narrow but it leads to life; Christ is the way and shows us by his very life how to run that way.

It is love for Christ that gives us the strength. Benedict tells us that the love of Christ must come before all else (RB 4.21; see 72.11). We are called to pray for our enemies out of love for Christ (RB 4.72). We are given the strength to observe little by little Benedict's listing of all the degrees of humility "as though naturally, from habit, no longer out of fear of hell, but out of love for Christ," and we are promised that we will arrive at that perfect love of God which casts out fear (RB 7.67-69).

But we never forget that it is Christ who loved us first. We are "so confident in [our] expectation of reward from God that [we] continue joyfully [through all difficulties] and say, *But in all this we overcome because of him who so greatly loved us*" (RB 7.39; Rom 8:37, italics mine). This is the love that Paul describes in Romans 8:

> What will separate us from the love of Christ? Will anguish, or distress, or persecution, or famine, or nakedness, or peril, or the sword? As it is written: "For your sake we are being slain all the day; / we are looked upon as sheep to be slaughtered." No, in all these things we conquer overwhelmingly through him who loved us. For I am convinced that neither death, nor life, nor angels, nor principalities, nor present things, nor future things, nor powers, nor height, nor depth, nor any other creature will be able to separate us from the love of God in Christ Jesus our Lord. (Rom 8:35-39)

This is the love that has surrounded us from our birth. "What . . . is more delightful than this voice of the Lord calling to us? See how the Lord in his love shows us the

way of life" (RB Prol.19-20). What indeed is more delightful to us than the voice of one who loves us, and loves us
even to death, even into life? He has said, "I am the way
and the truth and the life." St. Benedict knows this is what
we long for.

> Seeking his worker in a multitude of people, the Lord
> calls out, *Is there anyone here who yearns for life and de-*
> *sires to see good days?* (Ps 34:13). If you hear this and
> your answer is "I do," God then directs these words
> to you: If you desire true and eternal life, *keep your*
> *tongue free from vicious talk and your lips from all deceit;*
> *turn away from evil and do good; let peace be your quest*
> *and aim* (Ps 34:14-15). (RB Prol.14-17)

Benedict puts Psalm 34 in the mouth of Christ to tell us how
to heed his invitation and run on the way toward the good
life. Then Christ makes a promise: "Once you have done
this, my *eyes will be upon you and my ears will listen for your*
prayers; and even before you ask me, I will say to you: Here I am
(Isa 58:9)" (RB Prol.18).[5] Christ is indeed one who listens!

What the wisdom literature tells us and Benedict reminds us is that Christ is the beginning and the end, the
alpha and omega. Christ is the one who calls us, the one
who answers us even before we ask, the way on which
we journey, and the one we long to meet at the end of that
long road. Christ is the Wisdom of God and the heart of
our Christian life.

---

[5] The eyes and ears are probably coming from Psalm 34:16, but see
2 Chronicles 6:40; 7:15; 1 Peter 3:12.

Consider

> What new insights do you have as you come to the end
> of this book?

> What wisdom will you take with you on your journey
> of life?

Prayer

> Lord, fill us with your Spirit
> that we may thirst for you alone, the fountain of wisdom,
> and seek you as the source of eternal love.
> Bring us all together to everlasting life
> with you, our Triune God who lives and reigns forever
> and ever.

Bibliography

Brecht, Bertolt. *Der kaukasische Kreidekreis*. Berlin & Frankfurt/ Main: Suhrkamp, 1955.

Brueggemann, Walter. *In Man We Trust: The Neglected Side of Biblical Faith*. Atlanta: John Knox Press, 1972.

―――. *The Message of the Psalms*. Minneapolis: Augsburg, 1987.

―――. *Theology of the Old Testament*. Minneapolis: Fortress, 1997.

Casey, Michael. *Strangers to the City*. Brewster, MA: Paraclete, 2005.

Chodron, Pema. "Joy," from *The Wisdom of No Escape*. In *Wise Women: Over Two Thousand Years of Spiritual Writing by Women*, edited by Susan Cahill, 377–79. New York: W. W. Norton & Company, 1996.

Cyprian. *De dominica oratione* (The Lord's Prayer). In *Saint Cyprian: Treatises*. Fathers of the Church 36. New York: Fathers of the Church, Inc., 1958.

de Waal, Esther. *Lost in Wonder*. Collegeville, MN: Liturgical Press, 2003.

Di Lella, Alexander, and Patrick Skehan. *The Wisdom of Ben Sira*. AB 39. New York: Doubleday, 1987.

Donovan, Mary Ann. *One Right Reading? A Guide to Irenaeus*. Collegeville, MN: Liturgical Press, 1997.

Dumm, Demetrius. *Cherish Christ above All*. Mahwah, NJ: Paulist Press, 1996.

The Ecumenical Grail Psalter. Chicago: GIA Publications, 2015.

Fry, Timothy, ed. *RB 1980: The Rule of St. Benedict*. Collegeville, MN: Liturgical Press, 1981.

Heschel, Abraham Joshua. *Man Is Not Alone: A Philosophy of Religion*. New York: Farrar, Straus & Giroux, 1951.

——. *Who Is Man?* Stanford, CA: Stanford University Press, 1965.

Kardong, Terrence. *Benedict's Rule: A Translation and Commentary*. Collegeville, MN: Liturgical Press, 1996.

Karris, Robert J. *Eating Your Way through Luke's Gospel*. Collegeville, MN: Liturgical Press, 2006.

Lane, Belden. *Walking the Bible: A Journey by Land through the Five Books of Moses*. New York: HarperCollins, 2001.

The Liturgical Psalter: Canticles. Chicago: Liturgy Training Publications, 1996.

McDonnell, Kilian. *Adam on the Lam*. Collegeville, MN: Saint John's Abbey, n.d.

Merkle, John C. *The Genesis of Faith: The Depth Theology of Abraham Joshua Heschel*. New York: Macmillan, 1985.

Miller, Arthur. "The Story of Adam and Eve." In *Genesis as It Is Written*, edited by David Rosenberg. San Francisco: HarperSanFrancisco, 1996.

The New American Bible, Revised Edition. Washington, DC: USCCB, 2011.

Sleevi, Mary Lou. *Women of the Word*. Notre Dame, IN: Ave Maria Press, 1989.

Squire, Aelred. *Asking the Fathers: The Art of Inspiration and Prayer*. Ramsey, NJ: Paulist Press, 1973.